VISIBLE AND VITAL

A Handbook for the Aging Congregation

Harriet Kerr Swenson

To a dear friend in the faith... God bless! Harriet

PAULIST PRESS
New York/Mahwah, N.J.

Library of Congress Cataloging-in-Publication Data

Swenson, Harriet Kerr, 1933-
    Visible and vital: a handbook for the aging congregation/by Harriet Kerr Swenson.
        p.   cm.
    Includes bibliographical references.
    ISBN 0-8091-3449-7 (pbk.)
    1. Church work with the aged. I. Title.
BV4435.S95   1994
259'.3—dc20   93-38870
                                                                        CIP

Published by Paulist Press
997 Macarthur Boulevard
Mahwah, NJ 07430

Printed and bound in the
United States of America

CONTENTS

iii

ACKNOWLEDGMENTS

I extend many thanks to the following persons of faith:

Professor Robert Pazmino who, by example and dedication to academic process, lifts up our understanding of Christian education.

Dr. Mary Luti who, as sensitive chairperson of Master of Arts Programs, recognizes laypersons' contributions as valid.

David Swenson who, as mid-life friend, mentor, companion and affectionate husband, personifies the kind of integrity that psychologists only talk about.

PREFACE

Aging congregation! How often have we heard this phrase with all its undertones of negativity, discouragement, dismay.

Hopefully, this handbook will alert churches to the reality of the situation, namely, the immense positive possibilities for every age group to carry God's word into the whole world. It is not the end when the church as we know it changes.

Awareness of the incredible human potential for building and lifting up the church can be the beginning of new hope, new relationships, and new kinds of learning, thus expanding our ministry of personal growth and community action.

INTRODUCTION

This study is specifically intended for the pastoral minister who seeks direction in approaching the elusive subject of aging. Unlike the traditional method that focuses attention on a single area of interest, this handbook pinpoints multiple but dominant subdivisions with the intent of spurring the concerned Christian to further investigation. Chapter headings reflect questions about aging often asked by members, thus reviving the educational role of the institutional church caught up in responsible inquiry. Each of the issues briefly touched upon calls for further study. Any exploration of increased longevity represents an overlap of such disciplines as sociology and psychology. This presentation highlights the religious significance of aging that other studies often ignore.

The denial of the existence, needs and involvement of the older adult—in spite of known demographics—is common, and suggests that the church, in particular, is having difficulty understanding its mission. This study recognizes the beginnings of concern as it gradually becomes tuned in to bits and pieces of information and misinformation. It highlights the church's need to reexamine its covenantal base of accountability to God and to all others. Recognizing the ministry of the church as teacher, witness, loving healer, and servant means moving from attitudes of pretense, denial, ignorance and pride, to being open to God's purposes in the world of the present. While the subject of aging has not been central to biblical studies or traditional doctrines it is helpful to recall universal themes of equality, caretaking and respect which easily apply. From there our job in the church becomes one of weeding out other applicable truths and struggling with God's message in our time. Often floundering in its acknowledgment and valuation of those in the later years of the God-given life cycle, the institutional church appears to need tools to aid in breaking down barriers of negativity and cultural power.

This handbook concept, drawing on the servant model of the church, based on Christ's witness as the Servant of God, implies responsibility for the welfare of others. This particular format provides easy access to basic areas of concern, which were chosen after extensive general research of the field, in addition to the writer's personal life experience within seven churches in five different geographic areas of the United States. These short chapters take a brief look at such issues as diversity, the changed understanding of work vs. leisure, the adult as capable learner/teacher, the updated understanding of words such as "wisdom," "maturity" and "caregiving," and the value of communal responses as well as heightened sensitivity to one's relationship with God. This study strives to reflect church-centered roadblock questions, internalized or subtly stated, such as: "Why don't 'they' help themselves?" "Does it matter where Mom lives?" Or, from an aging woman in our culture: "What's going to happen to me?" Not meant to be read as a continuous whole, this format is designed for easy usage. The leader perusing the church bookshelf for immediate need in the classroom and discussion group, or the new planning committee preparing programs for ministry with older adults, can browse here for helpful suggestions. The inclusion of occasional literary references, as well as informal references to universal personality types, hopefully add to its usefulness. It is ecumenical in focus.

Each short chapter closes with a simple resource idea for general church application. Some readers may choose to turn to the extensive bibliography.

1

GETTING CAUGHT IN CULTURAL NORMS

Vague references to the "greying of America" ruffle our cultural perspective. TV coverage and newspaper reporting are packed with clichés such as Social Security package and senior discount rates; magazines with full color ads that suggest the purchase of Geritol or other medicinal products stare back at us in waiting rooms and subway stations. How long can we ignore significance?

Trained by our culture—even in cartoons—to think "young," we still find we can no longer avoid the onslaught. Then again, why do we wish to ignore it? To bypass "the last for which the first was made"? Have we been programmed to believe that aging is *only* loss? Has our culture taught us that aging is *only* a downhill battle, the foe disease, decay and death? Where are the advantages or gains? Why is the church often silent about such issues?

When historians began to explore what happened to make our view of aging what it is they found a great deal of ambivalence. In a culture where children were once seen as mini-adults,[1] where doctors prescribed medicines not according to age-specific needs,[2] where early New Englanders didn't seem to care how old they were,[3] and where debates over whether intelligence declines still reign, there were also other signs. Sermons[4] pointed to special virtues of the aged, and special affection seemed to abound between the elder and grandchildren.[5]

Historian David Fischer claims that *before* 1820 elders were exalted and feared, but that after the Civil War, along with industrialization, came the increased glorification of youth.[6] By the turn of the century, when older adults seemed to become a problem, forty-seven years was viewed as the average normal life span! Although the White House Conferences on Aging eventually addressed some concerns, the myths about aging continue to direct and subtly control thought and policy.

One list[7] of misinformation highlights the problem for us: The myth that all elders age in like manner (we actually become more diverse), the myth of un-productivity (paid employment is only one criterion for active involvement in life), the myth of disengagement (that all elders prefer separation from mainstream living is still being argued), the myth of inflexibility (elders are surprisingly adaptable to change), the myth of senility (unfair use of one word to describe often treatable conditions), and the myth of serenity (elders bear more stress than any other age group). Add to this the common language of our culture. A lengthy collection of derogatory words meaning "old" was also gathered by a Frank Nuessel, revealing our continuing negative attitudes.[8] Words included were: geezer, decrepit, hag, coot, over-the-hill, dirty old man. While none of us wants to be told we act or look old, neither do we know when, exactly, we qualify! What is old, anyway, besides cheese or furniture?

Who is "old" reflects a particular era or period in time. Now, it is generally defined as beginning at age 65, a chronological point in time which the government decided was to be the age for mandatory retirement. (This was changed to age 70 in the year 1978). The original declaration was followed by feelings of outrage by those who felt forced out of the labor force before they were ready. Other definitions of "old" followed, the most familiar from sociologist Bernice Neugarten who made a distinction between the young-old and the old-old. The former (ages 55–75) are those still active and able to maintain relative independence, whereas the latter (age 75 and older) are more vulnerable to physical and social limitations. As the population numbers increased and the life span lengthened, many other subdivisions of "old" were defined. These, in turn, eventually brought attention to those over age 85, the frail elderly, the 3.3 million who make up the fastest growing age group in the country.[9] This phrase will continue to pop up before us as the fast-growing statistics propel us into the twenty-first century.

Actually, contrary to public knowledge and, probably in part thanks to fear, denial, economic panic, and negative media coverage, only 5 percent of those aged 65–85 go into the dreaded nursing home environment.[10] Thus, an immense majority are apparently someplace else—but where? Being often out of sight, and feeling marginalized, these millions should raise questions in our minds. First, there are the easier questions such as: Could leisure become, not a blessing but a curse? After the gold watch is ceremoniously given, could one get tired of playing golf daily?

Then, in a rapidly changing economic system the questions multiply. How does anyone choose a place to live? Does the Bible have any messages that are helpful for the elder? Do "they" wish to be active or inactive in our churches? What exactly does satisfy when there is no Friday paycheck?

When all the evidence is in we can no longer deny the needs and uncertainty of elders in our culture. But the institutional church has plenty of concerns already on the agenda. It is in a precarious position, questioning survival. There are worries about membership, paying salaries, increased maintenance costs, changing neighborhoods, competitive programming, drugs. We could go on and on. The surplus of aged adults seem to be just another uncertainty when we want answers and solutions, not delayed speculation. Change is not welcome. But, to continue with the assumption that all elders are like Grandma Rose or Uncle William would be faulting the glaring truth surrounding us...the cozy church suppers with Bea's baked beans or Hattie's succulent pie have already been replaced by hard work at soup kitchens for the homeless; the Sunday School can't find enough teachers; the choir now pays its soloists because volunteers are lacking and, somehow, the increased number of elders in our ranks appear to be part of the problems. Could God be speaking to us? God is known for encountering us directly or through the lives of others. But, accustomed to reliance on self, maybe we don't want to hear about Someone else in control.

Life and death are part of God's mysterious gifts to us, and having recently been taught increased awareness of death and dying, perhaps we are now called to take a closer look at what it means to live as we age. Our knowledge of God is based on experience—our own, and what others share with us. At this point even more difficult questions surface. Knowing that, contrary to cultural messages, millions over age 65 are *not* sick, helpless or institutionalized, what are the implications for our churches? Could it be that aging is earmarked as God's method of presenting the opportunity for new kinds of learning to persons of every age?

As the elder experiences losses of friends, health and identity, the church, too, must acknowledge its own identity crisis. With our tendency to view the church as only a visible institution on the corner, we may need to remember it constitutes a gathering of believers who witness to the powers of God's love and grace available to every age. The church is, in essence, invisible, and the death of God's son on the cross for us changes our basic purposes from self-gratification and fulfilling of duties to positive responses out of loving choice. We are open to the various needs of the other because we are more than a volunteer organization. We have been commanded to love as God loved us.

The church is the place where values are transmitted, faith is nurtured, the will of God is taught, and where, in remembrance, we take part in ritual acts together. It is through the church that God calls us all to adoration and services beyond that of immediate family, personal goal or monetary gain. It is where we all search for answers to God's will in our lives, knowing God is revealed in events and situations in the past and will continue to do so in the future. It is there that we are called to remember God's ministry to the sick, and to the men and women of every age and race. It is there, after acknowledgment of sin and after repentance, that a new kind of life is offered. The elder often feels abandoned and that is why members embody the love of God, giving assurance that nothing can separate them from this love.

We cannot allow the aging adult to be falsely defined by cultural standards. With God's help, we can have the inner perceptions to view: *what* can be the benefits of purposeful living, *who* exactly are the valued holders of faith experiences, and *how* lovable, unique individual others still change and joyfully become free to turn inward, discarding the trappings of convention.

But cultural stereotypes and myths do not die easily. We in the church must move from seeing the many aged as symbols of loss, to asking instead, what God's message is. Loss is, after all, central to our Christian faith. Suffering on the cross brought new heights of meaning.

Although we mouth the belief that all persons are created in the image of God, it is in our actions that love will be known. When we take pride in knowing only things like the fastest route to McDonald's, it may be time to catch our breath and reevaluate. Believing that God has a purpose for all creation, let us go on to ask the most pertinent questions.

Suggested Reading:

Why Survive? Robert Butler

How Does It Feel to Be Old? Norma Farber

Church Resource #1: Dream List

- Our church at 29 Elm has excellent acoustics and handicap access.

- Our elders believe they are role models for the young and act accordingly.

- All elders are addressed according to their name preference.

- Transportation is provided at our church whenever needed.

- Elders feel welcome at all our functions.

- If the liturgy has been changed, the staff has made a special effort to explain, incorporate, or provide alternatives.

- The elders experience a sense of family within the church.

- The adult members of all ages participate in local agencies, and interfaith projects that support elder needs.

- Elders are consulted and asked directly about opinions, concerns.

- The members of the congregation are always on the alert for public and ecclesiastical policy that obscures individual need.

- The elders feel reasonably important to the congregation yet show modesty and restraint as to control or dictation of policy.

- The church welcomes all anonymous bequests marked for elder needs.

- All members treat all members as whole persons.

- The negative stereotypes associated with aging have been acknowledged and overcome.

- The church supports a nearby extended care facility. This does not mean merely donations; it means regular monitoring of elder needs.

- Study opportunities exist for theological and ethical bases of caring.

2

CONFIRMING THE STRENGTH OF DIVERSITY

Who is the elder in our church? *She* sits in the front pew, hat noticeably askew, yet melts away into the crowd before the closing hymn. Who is she?...*He*, midweek, is spotted ably aiding your child in crossing the street. You saw *her* (slouched there in the doctor's waiting room) because of the unmatched socks. Or what about *that* batch of grey-haired folk graciously serving limitless goodies after the Sunday worship? The same ones that provided inconspicuous help when your mother died?...Or, what about the last committee meeting when that retired gentleman in the faded plaid gave a well-thought-out defense of the latest policy skirmish? Who was *he*? New in town?...On the way home you ponder briefly about that widow at 17 Elm. Why does *she* live alone when there are all those places?...In the mail on the table is a letter from Aunt Sally, aged 74, saying *her* white-water rafting trip had been invigorating!...As you pour a cup of tea, you are thankful you are not friend Kate, trapped in her own home caring for an incontinent father; *she* confided just yesterday about the church failing to understand why she dropped out. Is it any wonder that we are having difficulty?

The diversity of this age group defies definition, but it also reflects the diversity of God's creation. If we can admit it, what often endears them to us is not their conformity but their individuality, courage, and spunk. What we remember, often, is the spontaneous honesty, or the nursing home visit when we came away aware, in spite of our bumbling intentionality, that we had been on the receiving end, enriched by *their* authenticity.

On the other hand, although we can't admit it, perhaps we get angry because they don't fit into nice little categories, i.e., fulfill our expectations of them. We want them to make things easier for us in our busy lives.

Well, unlike other age groups with their almost predetermined, well-defined behavior characteristics, elders cannot easily be classified. It is important that we recognize this. The older adult cannot be categorized into assumed behavior; their long pasts represent more variables than in other groups. While certain common psychological traits may be subtly present in all older adults, environmental influences, or what we broadly call "age-related life crises," can vary considerably. Common psychological traits we easily recognize might include a preference for familiar things, and a change in the sense of time, while crisis situations (such as marital problems, economic setback, institutionalization, death of a spouse, retirement, physical loss, etc.) heavily differentiate how a life is lived out.

Sometimes the biographical anthologies on the market about the aged make it sound as if every elder can or must contribute in certain outstanding ways to be culturally acceptable or noticed by us. This can be unfair. The elder needs reassurance that "ordinary" is fine and acceptable. Each has unique gifts to develop and share. (We might take heart in the thought that in our studies of Old Testament figures we learned that God chose the unexpected—what we might even call a motley crew. Moses, for example, not only lacked confidence, he was a murderer!) Moreover, faith questions which remain unexpressed often underlie the older adult's perspective of uncertainty and lack of self-esteem.

It is popular today to look at life according to stages. This means some of us in the church are familiar with the theories of appraising individuals according to psychological/social standards. For example, Havighurst's particular developmental tasks of early middle and late adulthood may be known, or Erikson's eight stages of infancy, early childhood play age, school age, adolescence, young adulthood, adulthood, and old age may have a familiar ring. But are we in tune with the religious needs of particular age levels? Are there special times in life when faith seems unique? All stage theories recognize that individuals do not necessarily proceed successively through all stages; some people regress or advance faster than others—development is actually gradual and continuous.[1] Being aware of the successful completion of developmental tasks may be helpful, but do these theories go far enough?

As we make the effort to know any complex and unique member of our church, might we not want to know more about levels of faith, and what part the church holds as to member development?

The church is the place where Christian formation is nurtured; it is in the creeds, the stories, the worship practices, the interrelational structure of group activity that we learn from each other, regardless of age. It is in the church that we are shaped, where we search scripture together, where we help one another.

Regardless of age, there is always the capacity for more growth and more change, James Fowler, in his *Stages of Faith*, points to the continual spiritual growth potential of every human being, according to stages that are "hierarchical, sequential and invariant." At the same time, with the dominance of our secular individualism, the elder not only gets caught in our cultural expectations, but in negative self-concepts which block awareness of life as a pilgrimage with and before God. Often unfamiliar with possible helpful technical knowledge about human development and, strongly influenced by inherited and familiar practices of self-reliance, as well as moralistic teachings that once provided the backbone to church and community, the elder today is in a difficult place.

The older adults of recent generations know of few role models for an extended life span. They often feel abandoned by family and friends. They often experience isolation and must live on fixed incomes. They need services, yet want to remain independent; they can be justifiably confused by the sometimes gracious, sometimes cruel environment. While the worst fear of the grandparent may have been the shame and ostracism of the county poorhouse, the worst fear of this age group is an extended illness creating a burden/expense to loved ones. But, while health and financial issues are real, what about the internal struggles related to spiritual well-being and the many subtle power issues that remain strong? These could include: when should one give over property, when is intervention necessary, and when it is, by whom?

In spite of our cultural messages of fear and decline, the real elder, not the stereotype, functioning without guidebook, continues to give evidence of courage. In the adapting and the confronting, many find miraculous ways of coping and transcending that could be shared with or taught to us! What we can learn from them includes increased freedom to be ourselves. What the neighbors (the culture) think may for us also become less important. What they may give to us is a statement such as, "I wear what is comfortable, not what designers tell me." What we could give to them is a climate for sharing meaning. The church is the place where what one wears or how one acts out one's life is accepted.

We are all confused about the meaning of "aging well." There are bound to be conditions for doing so, often attributed to economics. But with the diversity we can at least "expect to see multiple pathways to subjective well-being."[2] Within our churches we might even come to see that "one of the gifts of the later years is being Eucharist to others, to nourish others from the riches of one's personal experience of brokenness and blessing."[3]

Church Resource #2: Anthologies, Short Stories, and Other Works Portraying Strength of Diversity

Berman, Philip, *Courage to Grow Old*

Blythe, Ronald, *View in Winter*

Fisher, M.F.K., *Sister Age*

Fowler, Margaret, ed., *Songs of Experience*

Kohn, Martin, et al., eds. *Literature and Aging; An Anthology*

McFadden, Steven, *Profiles in Wisdom: Native Elders Speak About the Earth*

Martz, Sandra, ed., *When I Am An Old Woman I Shall Wear Purple*

Merriam, Sharan, ed., *Themes of Adulthood Through Literature*

Myerhoff, Barbara, *Number Our Days*

Painter, Charlotte, *Gifts of Age*

3

TARGETING THE MIDDLE-AGED PARISHIONER

Recognizing that the elder of today has been unprepared and has suffered accordingly, what can we do to ease the path of those approaching the same predicament? It was the Girl Scouts who thrived on being prepared! Dare we speak from the shoulder to the middle-ager, the member of another segment of the population that has already been targeted by cultural stereotypes about identity crises, or being man-in-the-middle? Copying the elementary teacher's slogan concerning reading readiness, can we give the middle-aged person admonitions as to elder "readiness," knowing "a wise man [sic] will have his Shepherd chosen and his fidelities fixed before he enters that trying decade"?[1]

Let's look at the common experiences of persons now aged 40–65. Chances are they are at the height of their careers. They are raising families. They find themselves sandwiched between demands of growing children and aging parents. There can be marital difficulties, including divorce with all its ramifications; there may be financial problems or traumatic job changes. With the home, family, job and community benefiting from the active and often powerful role of the middle adult, we might surmise that she or he would be the first to recognize the value of planning or organizing for the future.

But there is more. The typical middle-ager is ripe for serious thinking. Caught up in those multiple roles within family, office and community activity, she or he has also already felt—in scattered moments—frightening flashes of uncertainty and discontent. These people are at a crossroads. Interior questions loom, such as: Is it possible life is really half over? It is clear that she or he will not now be able to finish or complete certain precious dreams once conceived. It is at this time, as Maitland says so well, that "we need a vision more compelling than the pursuit of success....It is the need for a Christian vision of God."[2] It is a need to know a God who accepts us as we are. Our self-absorption, our achievement motivation, and our resistance to God's will is seen in our grandiose efforts and plans at mid-life to save ourselves. An awakening to ourselves as sinful and inadequate means that we are really open to God's voice, promising mercy, forgiveness and wholeness.

New possibilities within issues of suffering and loss may be examined and lifted up. Such confrontation will make the remainder of life's journey easier for all. For example, while the idea of blocks of leisure may seem attractive to Tom Brown, busy executive rushing daily for the commuter train, can he not be brought to a realization that a second, less harried career may await him later? How can he start now to prepare in some way, i.e., take a course, set aside funds, anticipate a hobby that can later expand into a satisfying, less harried occupation? On the other hand, the middle-ager—in avoidance of getting older—may not be able to hear or heed advice or warnings. How do we catch his ear about cultivating the use of time in preparation for intangible and less physically oriented living? Are there teachable moments?

It is, again, a simple question of planning and motivation. Much of what we become is based on what we have been. The habits established; the remembered responses to crises or transitional periods generally affect and remind us how we may behave in the future. Scrooge, of the famed Christmas tale, is our best known example. Unless a specific situation opens our hearts and minds to the possibility of transformation, we will remain as we have been. If we were fault-finders at age twenty-one, chances are that's what we'll be at eighty-one...unless—something is missing here. Aside from doing our part in making choices, doesn't our Christian faith say something about unde-served grace and possibility of Spirit? Aren't we nurtured, taught, guided, by a power beyond ourselves?

A Christian educator defines two primary tasks of mid-life.[3] In summary, they are Erikson's word "generativity" and reappraisal. According to James Fowler generativity means "an adult person having found ways through love and work, creativi-ty and care, to contribute to the conditions that will provide the possibility for members of the oncoming generations to develop their personal strengths at each stage."[4] This is a big job. Some experience an early awareness of generativity. This is seen in the fact that many adults choose and enjoy volunteer work. Others make a leap from a middle-aged focus on personal achievement to an understanding of life's value being found in how we influ-ence others before and after death. Any reappraisal of one's past, though painful, can be beneficial. Both generativity and reap-praisal can heighten awareness of life's purpose.

Consider the care of the physical body. The middle-ager, surrounded by scientific claims of moisturizing creams, best-selling books about life extension, and bizarre sounding treat-ments dependent on sheep-fetus injections,[5] is already making choices. (We like to think that in America we are on the right track.) But while we snicker at secular ways of prolonging human existence, we might remember that a major perspective is being confronted.

In a time of raised awareness as to beneficial health care issues, we can to some degree influence how we grow older by making positive changes in our life-styles. New knowledge besieges us about low-salt, less-fat diets, and orders to add more fiber while decreasing caloric intake. The elimination of smok-ing has been loudly proclaimed as has the existence of many brands of multivitamins. The value of reasonable exercise has been proven to contribute positively as to *how* we live out our extended life stages. Many illnesses and medical conditions associated with aging are preventable, though the voluntary nature of application of any of this can be limiting.

All options may not be as easy. Choices on a deeper level must also be made. According to Peck[6] these challenges include the need to value wisdom instead of physical power, and learning to develop mental flexibility as opposed to mental rigidity. In other words, we still can change, not only habits concerning the body, but can adjust and discern certain existing attitudes or known patterns of behavior. This is more difficult. Who, we ask, is going to lead the way? Teach? Empower? Jesus—as the wise preacher said—did not lecture the lost, he saved them...by example. This explains how we in the church can do our part. If, as Bianchi suggests, it takes a lifetime to formulate one's religious philosophy,[7] then it is never too late to touch the lives of others, mend our own ways or mold, in love, the future of middle-agers.

Consider our tendency to value self before others when, for example, we have been so glad to have that bright lawyer serve on our dwindling administrative committee that we have ignored his obvious health needs. Or, knowing that stress is a major characteristic of this age group, why do we pretend ignorance thereof? What can we do to acknowledge with them the existing problems, redirecting thought about values, priorities, and God's wishes for each of us—alone and together? "If there is a significant mid-life transition in which one's basic values undergo scrutiny and change, what does this suggest for classes and retreats aimed at mid-life adults?"[8] Are not many of the questions spiritual ones? An interesting workshop study was done with middle adults.[9] From this it was concluded that middle adults with a positive sense of purpose and meaning in their *own* lives held more positive attitudes toward life in general and toward elder Americans at large. So, what better time to build into our curriculum classes that relate to subjects that are on their minds, to benefit both their own lives and that of others?

For example, with the increased responsibilities of parental care, why not speak to the clashes of family rights and needs as common experiences to every member? Or, in the area of preventive services, why not education for retirement or shared learning for those experiencing empty-nest syndrome?

We in the church are the ones to bring to light the promise of God's presence (consider Romans 8:35). We are the ones who can aid in the choice of whether the middle-ager looks at the later years with what one educator[10] calls either anticipation or dreading. We effect choices.

Lastly, if awareness of finitude arises, how can the church respond? Can it go on denying that middle age gives us a unique time frame within which to order our living? Does the church need to witness to the fact that schemes for living forever are not more important than life eternal?

The questions we deliberately pose—such as "how do I wish to spend the balance of my life,"[11] without fear and according to whom, can make a difference. Whether it becomes the "dark night of the soul" or an opportunity for conversion may be up to us. What can be changed will be based on the power of the Spirit in our lives as we do our best to act out our communal faith. The big questions invite *all* of us to dig in.

To be 45 or 75 can be exciting. We can anticipate brand new perspectives in changes. The blessing is in knowing we have the time to prepare.

Suggested Reading:

Looking Both Ways, David Maitland

Nobody's Child: A Generation Caught in the Middle, Paul Irion U.C.C. Six Session Study

Church Resource #3: An Intergenerational Program

JANUARY Plan calendar of events within family context.

FEBRUARY Initiate monthly visitation to nursing homes.

MARCH Present dramatic production of members' lives. Base on tape interviews by Jr.–Sr. High.

APRIL Organize songfest for all tastes with commentary. Build in ballads, hymns.[12]

MAY Develop a diversified program for adult singles.[13] Elders as well as young adults make up this category.

JUNE Try a mock graduation for everyone. Rejoice, pray, over lesser known rites of passage such as retirement.

JULY Organize a clown ministry for use Sunday morning. World of costume and make-up has magic for all ages.

AUGUST Go on an all-family camping retreat.

SEPTEMBER Sponsor a Stone Soup Supper.[14] Choose a storyteller, mix soup, give proceeds to needy.

OCTOBER Offer a one-day workshop on learning together. Highlight differences and similarities.

NOVEMBER Young adults prepare turkey dinner for elders. Cooked by young married, served by youth, etc.

DECEMBER Celebrate rebirth with a video of year in review.

4

CHURCH PROGRAMMING AS EDUCATIONAL PROCESS

Christian Education takes on new and different status when one views the church as the best place for building whole-life preparedness. But, to see our church ministry to and with elders as primarily an educational process may need explanation and real intentionality.

We are talking here about programming across all phases and levels of church endeavor; those diverse kinds of experiences that can be avenues of learning and increased understanding. These will involve worship and fellowship, as well as more formal kinds of teaching by traditional methods. Careful planning on the part of the staff can lead to stimulation of thought and possibilities for growth within all age groups.

Specifically, to change our understanding of religious education from youth orientation to a concept of lifelong learning will not be easy. Religious learning has often meant designing classes for youngsters only, ordering reams of crayons and colored paper, and finding teachers either trained in kindergarten know-how, or with the physical stamina to keep up with teenage trends. It was the young only who needed to be taught; it was the young only who were thought capable of learning. But, mildly aware that cousin Fred got a doctorate at age 59 and that

Grandma is taking a night course in Italian, we have been led to suspect that something new is going on.

The good news is that the older adult *can* learn and *likes* to do so. Consider the amazing success of Elderhostel programs. Begun in the 1970s in New Hampshire, with the emphasis on short-term, low-cost courses on college campuses, the idea is now offered nationwide, as well as around the world! Consider also awareness that the once popular IQ intelligence testing—based on youthful responses—failed to include crystallized intelligence ability which evaluated knowledge learned through life experience.

Today, we know that though the pace of learning may be slower, and though situational barriers may hinder,[1] the older adult does learn and, in some cases, intelligence levels—beyond age 70—may even increase.[2] That adults are capable, intelligent people can be seen in the acceptance of erudite 17th century sermons, the popularity of the Chautauqua movement with its wide reach of audience, and the eventual development of evening classes for those holding daytime jobs. Now, with the increased longevity of our population, the church is in a position to recognize both the learning needs and the potential contributions of its growing aged membership.

One educator[3] reminds us that there are many ways of learning which we can incorporate into our churches. Aside from the random experience and the self-planned activity there is also the incidental learning, completed as a result of participating in an act within a formal setting. The self-planned may seem the most familiar to us (we all know those self-starter types who have, through hobbies or strong interests, developed entirely on their own, an expertise that surpasses formal training.) But what about this learning from participating? Moreover, instead of herding the elder to the sideline, why not include them in the inner working/planning mechanisms of the church programming? Ability will be shared and given, while the opportunity for his/her growth and learning is encouraged. The art and science of helping adults learn (andragogy)[4] can be a church goal, while leaders remember that only meaningful work will actually motivate. (This contrasts with the young adult who may, without genuine concern, learn facts merely for a degree program.) In addition, the elder, as Missinne[5] points out, is not simply devoting his life to finding meaning for himself; he also *gives* meaning. This reinforces Bianchi's finding in which, out of reflections on elderhood, many older adults offer what they have learned from life and what they would like to pass on to us. These are not facts about battles or birth dates. These are reminders such as learning to forgive oneself, finding happiness in the present moment, discovering worthwhile projects and remembering that overwhelming issues are not entirely new, because they have been faced and resolved before.[6]

Robert Butler suggests that any education *for* elders should include: 1) education for inner satisfaction, 2) education for pre-retirement, 3) education for post-retirement in senior centers and 4) education for societal utilization, i.e., special training such as job retraining.[7] In the light of this, might we not add the church as a place or ideal environment for some of this?

The small support group experience can be a popular starting place. Addressing a special need such as that of the widow facing grief could mean an informal group session with a trained leader, thus providing a non-threatening opportunity for shared ventilation and caring. For example, Ruth Jacobs, author and well-known regional group leader, guides older women into building up positive self-imaging.

Within the category of small group experiences, many churches provide one day or short-term class instructions as to the best methods of handling the tiresome paperwork associated with wills, banking and medical records. A difficult task at any age, this can be led by a retired lawyer from within the congregation. A paperback such as *In Time of Need* by Frank King, and published by Abingdon, is a workbook of business-related information to be compiled in advance of crisis, and, while as they say, the person is still of sound mind!

Not to be excluded, and outside the factual kind of knowledge is the necessity for education programs to recognize the value of intangibles such as common sense, reasoning, or versatility—all primary to later usefulness.[8]

All in all, there is little in the way of ready-made written materials for religious education departments. This means the church may choose to create what is needed. Faithful teachers have always found a way of doing what needs to be done. Although there is little curriculum for use with youngsters, art projects, such as calendars, have been effective, with children picturing favorite elders. These have been published and marketed locally at fair prices as fund-raisers by churches and local agencies.

The Christian way of relationship between age groups must be directly and indirectly taught, and the intergenerational approach can be one way to bring enrichment and surprise. Attitudes are learned. The assumption that children have, at home, quality experience with adults can be a myth. In fact, many come from one-parent families, and few ever see or interact with older adults such as grandparents. Therefore, planning educational events is in the realm of the church's teaching mission. The value of this can be seen in the following program. An intergenerational project between a Hebrew Home for the Aged and a small college meant that students saw forms of hope as the major trait of the elders, with their own experience of discovery a new process for them.[9] New kinds of learning experience can break away from rote learning yet include the reinstitution of the traditional.

Random ideas for beginning programming that will touch all ages might include: an annual focus on an aging theme within all church activities; the use of NCOA's literary booklets; Spafford's book[10] now on tape (Zondervan Audio Pages); any excuse for a celebration (anniversary? special event? since parties bring all ages together); chances for creative, artistic expression, as in poetry workshops; recording of elder history; literacy and second language programs (our multicultural society forgets special needs of elders from different heritages); retreats which focus on mid-life crisis or related issues such as second careers; Bible study as a search for explicit stories of justice and compassion involving the aged; the creation of ritual services for older adult transition periods;[11] the fun of a dramatic production.

A large scale interfaith project that has become a model nationwide, and which includes educational opportunities, is the Shepherd's Center Project in Kansas City, Missouri. Begun by a Methodist clergyperson, Elbert Cole, it is not a place but a process that really works! It is carried out by 25 churches in a 15 square mile area. It is based on elders serving elders and recognizes the importance of social interaction. It is intended for persons *not* in institutions, and while it supports independent living, it also provides older adults an opportunity to experience life satisfaction by participation in its many programs and services. Other programs to investigate might include older adult contemplative communities and two concepts shared by James Ellor.[12] One is called Senior Friends and is sponsored by a congregation that brings adults to those returning from the hospital. Practical aid is given, prayer and Bible study is shared. In turn, the aided person contributes when he or she recovers. The other, Gift of a Lifetime, is a Presbyterian program that uses older volunteers to develop local church programs for other older adults.

Any new programming within our churches will require effort, time, and much assessment and evaluation.

> The final approach to learning is problem solving with the necessary steps of: definition, isolate the options, test the consequences, decide on the course, plan the procedure of action, collect the resources, carry through the process, adjust to the obstacles, complete the action, evaluate.[13]

Hopefully, with all tools in gear, the renewed energy and commitment will transpose into: successful reeducating of teachers away from youth-only to a lifelong orientation; defining specific subjects useful to all ages; buying quality large-print materials; waking up to what other churches are also trying; developing competent lay leadership; finding outside funding for innovative programming; designing new intergenerational projects; adopting stances of inclusion and listening; discovering ways of being a factual information service; exhibiting sensitivity to those homebound who are ready to participate in new methods of involvement, and raising awareness of issues such as nutrition and abuse.

"The church can be a center of continuing adult education, with the power to change people's minds."[14]

The strange old man interviewed by the arrogant youth becomes transformed into a loving representation of "real" in the eyes of the teenager confused by culture's lessons; the wiggly child forgets her lines in the nativity scene play but experiences first hints of forgiving love in the sympathetic presence of front-row Grandma!

Suggested Reading:

Re-thinking Adult Religious Education. A Practical Parish Guide, Karen Szentkeresti and Jeanne Tighe

Teaching Older Adults, Linda J. Vogel

Church Resource #4: Films and Videos

A Day In The Life of Nancy Moore (Alzheimer's), 28 mins., Terra Nova Films, Chicago, IL

A Good Place To Grow Old, 24 mins., ASA, San Francisco, CA

Aging In A Rural Environment, 37 mins., Univ. of Guelph, Ontario, Canada

All Your Parts Don't Wear Out At The Same Time, 28 mins., Mass Media Ministries, Baltimore, MD

Company of Strangers, 100 mins., Canada

Cottonman, 30 mins., Terra Nova Films, Chicago, IL

Death of a Gaudy Dancer, 26 mins., Mass Media Ministries, Baltimore, MD

Every Day Counts, 20 mins., New Film Co., Arlington, MA

(In)Dignity of Aging, ESMA, Bethlehem PA

Just to Have a Peaceful Life (abuse), 10 mins., Terra Nova Films, Chicago, IL

Minnie Remembers, 5 mins., Mass Media Ministries, Baltimore, MD

Mr. Krueger's Christmas, 24 mins., Mass Media Ministries, Baltimore, MD

Old, Black and Alive, 30 mins., New Film Co., Arlington, MA

On The Aging Of Parents, Lutheran Center on Aging, Seattle, WA

Passage, 1 hr., New Film Co., Arlington, MA

Peege, 28 mins., Mass Media Ministries, Baltimore, MD

Rose By Any Other Name, 15 mins., Mass Media Ministries, Baltimore, MD

The Mailbox, 24 mins., Mass Media Ministries, Baltimore, MD

The Shopping Bag Lady, 21 mins., Mass Media Ministries, Baltimore, MD

Up Golden Creek, 18 mins., Presbyterian Pub. House, Atlanta, GA

Volunteer to Live, 30 mins., Shepherd's Center on Aging, Kansas City, MO

Weekend, 12 mins., Mass Media Ministries, Baltimore, MD

Women of Georgian Hotel, 20 mins., Terra Nova Films, Chicago, IL

5

GETTING STARTED

It is time for specifics. In youth we heartily sang the hymn, "It Only Takes a Spark," while in adulthood, more culturally programmed, we hesitate. At last, going to our library, we check out a copy of *Why Survive?* How did it get to be like this, we speculate? Accustomed to cheery bumper stickers, graffiti or third-rate telecasts for instruction, we turn on the tube, despairing, for a quick escape from the subject of aging.

It is not easy to stay "on the way." For the impulse on the part of the individual to become an effective, shared, Christ-centered venture will require concentrated effort, continued commitment, and shared involvement. It means becoming, like Jesus, the embodiment of God's grace, purposes and power.

Unlike most areas of study, the examination of aging—with its element of personal and cultural denial—requires preliminary clarification. Preconceived notions that are emotionally laden, or narrow definitions of what constitutes church "business," may need to be sorted out. Just because somebody's cousin George could use a meal brought in does not warrant leaping into a full scale group food plan. First, or fundamental, to caring or service...before any course of action can be taken... is the learning about one's own attitudes and assumptions about aging.[1]

If we anticipate that old age will be filled with misery, poverty, suffering, loneliness, and bitterness,

chances are greater that it will be so. When negative
expectations, fears, prejudices and stereotypes are
uncovered, their insidious effect on later life can be
diminished.[2]

An early planning session of volunteers at your church
could be devoted to exploring cultural or inherited viewpoints
about aging. This could easily be done using a short self-quiz[3] or
an opinion survey compiled by the acting leader about commonly held beliefs. Discussion could follow, revealing much to the
self, as well as to the future relevancy of the group.

Second, finding the best permanent leader for the chosen
enterprise is central, even though it may be difficult. Definitions
of what makes a quality leader have changed over time. Within
the early church there appears to have been diversity of title and
responsibility—from overseers to prophets and teachers. Today,
qualities such as glamor and productivity, often associated with
getting ahead, are often cited. The emphasis for leadership
development is apt to be on psychological methods for improv-
ing self-confidence, or determining what motivates people.
Several ways to achieve success, according to one contemporary
leader, include: a willingness to face risks, be innovative, have
high expectations, maintain a positive attitude, and get out in
front.[4] We would do well to apply such positive features within
our church context.

Within our western culture we seem to have problems with
authority figures, that is in both wanting and resenting advice
and guidance from other sources. Within our churches, however,
the thirst for leaders who are open to the leading of the Holy
Spirit is especially applicable. As someone once said, the church
that calls for a cruise director will get exactly that! Or, within
our churches we may not want to hear what is currently being
said about the quality of leadership. For example, one critic
states that if insights from modern biblical scholarship are not
taught, if psychology becomes a substitute for religion with its

leaning toward non-directional training and, if ministers are unable to be self-critical, thus leaning toward overly-protective leadership, our churches become malnourished.[5]

Religious professionals are reluctant to get involved with older adults for the following reasons: tight time schedules, criticism from older adults who are no longer active in the church, a feeling of helplessness in responding appropriately to certain issues, pressures from the congregation to recruit young couples and young families, and feelings of guilt for not spending more time visiting and providing more pastoral care.[6]

But those of us starting new programs or organizing committees in areas of concern must not assume that clergy are the only potentials for leadership. An elder within the membership may be the real potential for direction. Many leaders in the Old Testament were advanced in years—Moses was 80 when he led Israel out of Egypt, and Abraham was 75 when he headed for Canaan.

A keen observation reminds us that our elders are our greatest reservoir of experience, capable of consultant status at all levels. Imagine a church including 100 older members with an average membership being 37 years. Multiplied, this adds up to an experience bank of 3,700 years! Such extensive backgrounds would include familiarity with problem solving and influences from contact with strong leaders.[7]

Good leadership doesn't, of course, always pop up. Chances are it may need to be not only equipped with information but nurtured spiritually.[8] Leadership within our churches can mean a calling—a response to God, an unsophisticated wanting to participate in bringing God's kingdom to earth. Thus the elder's style, in particular, may bear different marks than that of the secular boss. 1) She or he may exhibit power by simply speaking out of life experience, 2) may unconsciously or humbly be showing direction without intention, 3) may use standards of wisdom and virtue that on the surface appear not to apply but on closer inspection or experience prove to be valid. She or he may be aware that needed power comes not from the self but from One above. All this brings to mind the similarity to Jesus' methods and the fact that fruition of any kind requires communal interaction.

After leadership has been found, there can still be confusion as to where to begin. While your initial committee may be full of ideas about programming (they are limitless—from matching older volunteers with disabled children to forming friendly visitation groups), the organizing must be in place. Hopefully, accustomed to planning other ventures, most churches will know the usual way to proceed. If not, here are two approaches.

First, a five-step plan such as the following can be easily utilized. Briefly, define the problem, establish the goals and objectives (including identifying any alternative approaches), develop the program, implement the plan, and then later evaluate.[9] With each church varying in size, tradition, theological base and geographical location,[10] the work ahead calls for a thoughtful approach or adaptation. Groans of "not another meeting!" may be heard, but calls to legitimate tasks always bring forth the faithful. Remember, educators in high places are having difficulty making the transition from youth focused programming to an adult or intergenerational ministry, so do not fret. Awareness of being led by the Spirit can mean that others will join when momentum is achieved.

The steps for developing the program and implementing the plan have been presented in chapter 4 of this study, while step five, evaluation, is briefly addressed in the conclusion of this chapter. However, here are a few comments about steps one and two. Identifying the special needs of the older adult in the congregation can be easily accomplished. Churches can draw up their own questionnaires to determine the interests and needs of the older members, or they can use one of the many printed forms in denominational publications. Of course, a personal visit to each elder to acquire the detailed answers will ensure better and more responses. The results tallied can be very helpful in the choice of specific programs of action.

Note: Churches have been pleasantly surprised to learn about specific courses of action already in place! In addition, we tend to forget that a major course of action could be focused on changing children's negative attitudes. (This was suggested after someone disguised herself as an elder, experiencing firsthand our cultural negativity).[11]

The establishment of goals—as suggested—might mean following the membership survey with a community one. This ensures that time and energy are not wasted in duplicating existing programs of service. This reinforces awareness of the basic needs of *all* other adults. What is found may seem to be common knowledge, but many of us, caught up in our own pressing personal needs, can be unaware of the basic needs of others. For example, we may be familiar with our changes of transportation needs through time—from van to station wagon to two-door compact—but do we know that Mable, living on the outskirts, has no access to transportation of any kind? Or, as part of some close-knit family, are we aware that many live alone, without contact with a single, living relative or friend? Blaine Taylor's words about need are a gentle reminder. You will find they need the same essentials you do:

> to be loved
> to be taken seriously as persons
> to be listened to and accepted for what they are
> to be active doing interesting things
> to be really needed by at least one other person
> to be occupied with concerns other than self
> to be responsive in faith to the Lord Jesus Christ.[12]

In her book on adult religious education, Linda Vogel shares another perspective concerning levels of needs. These are based on Maslow's hierarchical ones. These four areas, so helpful for intentional ministry, relate to: life maintenance, life enrichment, life reconstruction and life-transcendence.[13] Life maintenance points to the basic essentials such as food and shelter. Life enrichment denotes an opportunity to develop skills or experience intellectual growth. Life reconstruction means reordering life after a crisis such as divorce or the death of a spouse. Life transcendence implies connecting life stories to the meanings of the teachings of the church. These suggest specific direction that new programming can take after need surveys are evaluated.

The second approach for getting started is based on questions.[14] These could include: What is the purpose of the new project? Will it be formal or informal? What is the timetable? Where will the program be set up? If even more help is needed, perhaps a film could be reviewed and shared.

Resources to supplement possible needs are available but may be difficult to locate. With the areas of concern with aging so vast, it will take a dedicated committee to identify and collect the initial information, before any appropriate action can be started.

Outside our local church there are increasing numbers of persons who can help. National boards are in the process of training individuals to serve as gerontology consultants for their churches. Also, outside our local churches, we have access to denominational publications. Most agencies and departments have compiled a reasonable amount of information. They have also recently written policy statements that can inform and clarify. The Methodist Church, for example, has formed a very active Advisory/Coordinating Committee on Older Adult Ministries that holds exciting annual convocations and publishes a monthly News and Notes update on aging; ESMA, a longstanding volunteer agency of the Episcopal Church, offers a wide range of inexpensive materials for church ministry and programming to, with, and for the elder; the American Baptist Church has a full-time advocate on the national level in the person of Dr. Carol

Pierskalla, director of *Aging Today and Tomorrow,* and current chair of NICA.

Requests to denominational offices for material are welcomed. Personal contact can also initiate new or better responses on their part. Recommendations as to speakers, methods of program development, successful programs already in progress, as well as notification of dates and times of inspirational workshops in your region, may come as a wonderful surprise. Sometimes, these aids cross denominational lines or lead to resources in your immediate vicinity.

There are also large scale secular groups that can be helpful. These include national organizations like The National Institute on Aging, The National Council of the Aging, and the Administration on Aging. The American Association of Retired Persons (AARP) not only has a significant number of publications available for the asking, but their helpful monthly publication *Modern Maturity* is mailed to all its members. It also maintains an interreligious liaison office with a helpful and dedicated staff.

There are a significant number of college and university research centers in the country that are regularly publishing their new findings. They will provide us much new information in the future. Though often focused on secular or purely scientific data, what is learned often overlaps our related concerns. Especially significant in the field of active religious research is the Center on Aging at the Presbyterian School of Christian Education in Richmond, Virginia. Specific large scale and well-known programs and ideas can stimulate local efforts.

Consider:

Never Too Late: brings continuing education programming to homebound older adults. (City Community College of City University of New York.)

Generations Together: employs older adults in child care. (University of Pittsburgh.)

Babbitt Aging Resource Library: provides books, magazines and film material to large geographic areas thanks to a generous donor.

Sage (Senior Actualization and Growth Exploration): proves that not only youth benefit from techniques such as meditation and biofeedback.

IRP (Institute for Retired Professionals): provides teaching and learning opportunities within education programming.

Important at the beginning stage of any program is the visible enthusiasm and commitment of its committee members. If the venture is to be widely effective, all kinds of promotional work must be done. Letting the congregation know that this ministry has started and that many are actively involved, can influence and add to its effectiveness. Again, do not forget that some of the most loyal and able supporters will come from the age group to which you wish to minister. As time moves on and results and responses of various kinds flow in, new questions will arise.

Evaluation, or the final stage of any plan, must take place. While we may be aware of what other churches have done or are doing, we may not yet be familiar with all the options. The prayerful addressing of both pitfalls and successes may require new tactics. Clearly, new recommendations or new issues may need to be addressed. Continued investigation will be required in such a new field of research, concern, and glaring need. Be patient. As to church programming and process at all levels, God, our " designated" leader, will show the way.

Suggested Reading:

Older Adult Ministry: A Resource for Program Development—
the Presbyterian Office on Aging, the Episcopal Society for

Ministry on Aging, the United Church Board for Homeland Ministries.

Affirmative Aging: A Resource for Ministry. Study Guide available. Episcopal Society for Ministry on Aging (ESMA).

Church Resource #5: Simplified Church Survey Form

The _____Committee at _____Church is currently contacting all older adults in anticipation of developing better relationshiops with its members.

Please fill out this short form. Anything you share with us will remain confidential.

NAME _____

ADDRESS _____APT#_____

_____

TELEPHONE _____

I am   ❑ single   ❑ widowed   ❑ divorced   ❑ married

I live with_____❑ no one

I would welcome assistance with:

      ❑ transportation   ❑ home repairs   ❑ meals

      ❑ daily phone call   ❑ paperwork   ❑ other

I have the following skills I would like to share:

_____

These are the kinds of church programs that would be helpful and in which I could participate:

_____

I need more information about:

      ❑ day care   ❑ respite care   ❑ medical discounts

      ❑ SS benefits   ❑ housing   ❑ new church programs

      ❑ other _____

Mr/Mrs. _____will call to verify the best time to visit you and will collect the form.

                                          THANK YOU

6

EMPOWERING DISCIPLESHIP

An elder speaks to us:

> Older folks today make up what might be called the
> "far-too-long-silent generation." Seldom have we
> stood up for our rights, which were earned over a life-
> time of working and giving and sharing, nor have we
> been critics of a society in which others suffer from
> inequality and lack of opportunity. Our sizable minor-
> ity of 30 million is far too unprotesting and acquies-
> cent. Rather than becoming the powerful moral and
> political force we could be, we have, for the most
> part, remained silent spectators of what was going on
> around us.[1]

We in the institutional church may add to the above a "yes, get
crackin." If there are so many of you, then speak up, stand up,
defend yourself. But we are often unaware of the obstacles they
confront.

Obstacle one: We forget that those of another age group
have been influenced by different factors.[2] These include politi-
cal, environmental, economic, social and familial, as well as
many unexpected life events, and how one culturally responded.
Chances are that those in the active 65-plus bracket, brought up
to remain mute about most things, will interpret the mere

thought of speaking out as making a public spectacle. To suffer in silence has been generally the accepted cultural norm of this particular group, though there are always exceptions. Women's experience of this is seen in Marge Piercy's poem "*Unlearning to Not Speak.*" Those of a younger generation—such as those socially active in the 1960s—when aging, will hopefully exhibit a totally different response to the current marginalization. More educated, more worldly-wise, they will probably be instrumental for beneficial change. In the meantime, we hear repeatedly "Why bother?" or "What can one do?" in the context of hearing an older neighbor committing suicide, or a governmental social security cut that is in the making. The thought of solidarity as power is unfamiliar and not understood as possible or probable.

Obstacle two: The elder's view of the self differs from the public one.[3] How can we in the church change that? How can we help empower the elder? When much of the way "she" feels about herself as she ages was taught by her environment—meaning her neighborhood, her community and church; when she can no longer wear a size ten dress like the one in the store window and therefore stays home from worship; when she sees gray in her hair and believes the only way to be acceptable is to change the color; when she resigns from the church board because no one ever values her occasional contribution and falls into that victim or "wrinkled baby" stance, what will *we* do?

In real life, a few have paved ways for speaking out. Maggie Kuhn of Gray Panther fame and Lou Cottin are among them, though some of us can remember society's derogatory remarks about older adults like Eleanor Roosevelt who broke the elder silence.

Well,…yes…we consigned many elders to such categories as ridiculous, fossil, etc. (Consider the study[4] of 265 articles on aging which showed that many readers held such negative images of older people.) We wanted them to be passive, polite, silent, irrelevant. We were not ready for them to be visible, verbal and vehement representatives of our culture. Those who dared to defy convention felt our wrath, and the elder tended to withdraw into accepting our definition of them.

Obstacle three: Though the seed has been sown, another obstacle to their empowerment remains: Ourselves. Thus the call is to righteous indignation and active participation.

> The task of re-establishing the validity of the elderly in this country is difficult. What is called for is determination. We must have faith in our own ability to lead the struggle for fundamental changes...the way we are perceived by younger Americans discredits us...the way politicians toss about our basic and general needs demeans us.[5]

To try to empower any group in any time period is difficult. And to bring an elder and the church to awareness of what may be a new role concept within our present pluralistic society, where those who need us are not necessarily our cousins in Jersey, calls for a new understanding of family. Often caught up in self-pity, worn out from earlier life stresses, feeling unable to deal with additional change, worried about basic survival issues of food, shelter, health or social isolation, the elder may adopt a stance of "enough" and "leave me alone."

Studies have shown that ability "to resist influence of negative stereotypes" is possible only when anxiety is reduced and "autonomy is sufficiently marked."[6] But new attitudes and behavior, once learned or adapted, can bring additional stress or adjustment. Consider the powerful book, *All Passions Spent,* by Vita Sackville-West. The main character was thought by society to be an obstinate old woman. She did not want to be taken care of by her children. She wanted to make her own decisions as long as possible—to maintain control—thus antagonizing those close to her, appearing disagreeable.

It will require strategy by the church and caring others to lead all ages to responsible reactions concerning cultural injustice. Once the obstacles are confronted, we can then ask directly: "How can we aid in identifying the gifts?" That someone who shuffles can be on the giving end of life may be a new thought to digest on the part of the questioner! The unique perspective of the older adult has promise.

There is no other age group that has had such a long period of real experience behind them. These people have survived untold numbers of wars, personal joys and sorrows; observed phenomenal industrial and scientific invention. They have the advantage of the "long view" on themselves, others, institutions—including churches—that can be helpful in the making of decisions and the planning of futures.

Then there are their skills, meaning a lifetime of work experience, perhaps specialized in one particular area. This abundance of expertise can nourish us here in our churches, our communities, our world.

Seldom recognized is the image of "holder of traditions." A role once of great value within oral cultures, it can be retrieved in the treasuring of special events and elements that have gone before.

The elder can also be our twentieth century prophet.[7] In a world badly in need of hope and renewal amidst so many kinds of injustice and pain, the elder can speak out from his or her advanced way of "seeing." Often caught up in the pressures of daily decisions and trivialities we tend to forget the bigger pictures. Such a stance for the elder can, as David Maitland suggests, mean a partaking of limitations as the beginning, not the end, of freedoms. Life on a plateau, as the individual shares, can be a place of, among other things, integration and consolidation, all without society's idea of constant change.[8] Less can mean more.

The overheard words of "he's a worker" in praise of another need not make a physically handicapped member feel unqualified. While the church's major approach in ministry with the older adults has mainly centered around social service programs and pastoral care, there is another important ministry. It is that of teaching wider responsibility to those still unaware of how they can "give of their seasoned abilities to the betterment of their communities...They are the greatest untapped resource in our society."[9]

What empowers a marginalized group to change? First, it means *not only* looking at externals but looking within. Only the institutional church as the body of Christ in the world can effectively address this. By teaching about holding a vision beyond themselves, by deliberate redefining vaguely held belief issues, by reincorporating the value of adult education, and by such methods as active inclusion and active listening the church can bring about significant outreach.

Second, a good beginning place for shared teaching and learning of these principles might be a concentrated look at wholeness and its implications for Christian living. This is clearly portrayed in a recent article[10] of the ***Generations*** publication. In summary, the author reminds us that in our "Judaeo-Christian tradition all human ties are based upon a prior and ongoing relationship with God as Creator, Sustainer, and Redeemer" and in the familiar instruction to love the Lord with our *whole* hearts, our *whole* souls, our *whole* minds, our *whole* strength, followed by the instruction to love our neighbors as ourselves (Mark 12:28–31). This command to wholeness, he observes, contrasts with our custom of viewing elders as only declining bodies, and suggests *only* elders may be able to understand the concept.

Third, it is clear that many elders would like to serve, but have not been prepared![11] We must help in the preparation.

Fourth, we can also listen. Listening is something that can be taught and learned, and recent trends make us realize it is a skill to be used and sharpened. To hear the pain, not to run from it, can be part of our new commitment practiced together. This role of the church—this not-easy opening of doors of relationship—will promote interdependence and direction for shared tasks.

Fifth, by making every effort to include those of all ages into our programming, by enabling within common goals, by celebrating within liturgical expression, as well as special social occasions, by listening to what is said verbally and nonverbally, we proclaim our acceptance of elders as persons, and obey God's word for the world. In turn, they, too, learn to live for others. Though the body may be slowing down, the heart and soul may be mysteriously tuned to the best of ways.

The dictionary defines "empower" as the ability to give power or authority; to authorize. We in the church know that by our presence and involvement in elders' lives, we release reminders of God's activity in their memories, bringing new awareness of where Christ empowers us all.

The church's past transgressions, combined with their unintentional forgetfulness and limited awareness of gifts mark the opportunity for new witness and new life.

Suggested Reading:

Age Wave, Ken Dychtwald

Life in the Afternoon, Edward Fischer

Church Resource #6: Empower By Building a Library of Usable Books for All Needs

Curry, Cathleen, *When Your Spouse Dies* (help for those who grieve)

Daly, Eugene, *Thy Will Be Done* (guide for elders re wills, taxation, etc.)

DelBene, Ron, et al., *When An Aged Loved One Needs Care* (short booklet of helpful facts)

Fischer, Kathleen, *Winter Grace* (late-life spirituality in easy-to-read format)

Gray, Ruth, *Survival of the Spirit* (true account of detour through retirement home)

Lessing, Doris, *Diaries of Jane Somers* (adult literature; woman's experience of caregiving)

Morgan, Richard, *No Wrinkles on the Soul* (devotions for elder use)

Myerhoff, Barbara, *Number Our Days* (famed study of urban Jewish ghetto aged)

Nouwen, Henri, *Aging*

Sapp, Stephen, *Full of Years* (biblical exploration)

Spinelli, Eileen, *Somebody Loves You, Mr. Hatch* (juvenile: ages 4–7)

Seuss, Dr., *You're Only Old Once* (adult humor in picture and verse)

7

LOOKING AT THE RELIGIOUS LIFE OF OLDER ADULTS

Some of us treasure memories of the way our parents carried out their faith. Some of us are afraid any direct inquiry as to belief will bring an emphatic "none of your business." Others, if not careful, may make broad generalizations based on only close first-hand observance. For example, Grandpa Jenkins—besides his daily shredded wheat for breakfast, likes: 1) to sing *all* the verses of the Sunday morning hymns, and 2) does not like to sign those pesky new-fangled pledge cards! Therefore, as we in the church take a closer look at the elders now in our midst, questions arise. What has influenced what we now see? What has changed? What remains important? What can we observe without getting bogged down in word-game arguments about religion?

The older adult has seen many changes in our churches. In fact, if we look back at congregational services within the American tradition, we *all* have reason to be surprised. The age distribution was once quite different: there were fewer elders and many children. The church was dominated by male leadership, though the women worked industriously behind the scenes. By the 1950s there was liturgical reform along with the rise of the liturgical calendar or lectionary. This was followed by tensions between conservative and liberal interpretation.

While in earlier days the minister may have held the role of public official or minister to the entire town, he was primarily an overseer of morals. Once known to be a threefold scholar/preacher/visitor, he then came to see himself more as teacher than priest. Today, the one in ordained leadership leans less toward a studious and more toward an activist role—is caught up in many administrative duties—and probably chooses to spend a major allotment of time in pastoral counseling responsibilities.

These institutional changes are difficult for elders because change can be interpreted as death. Moreover, we have also seen the emergence and definition of women's spirituality which places new value on individual experience and relationships. Considering that women today live longer than men, does this point to other changes in our futures? Meanwhile, how the church deals with elders in faith practice, new situations, decision-making, and changed policy, requires real communication effort, skilled planning, and loving pastoral concern.

"It is neither accidental nor undesirable that old people constitute the majority population in churches," says David Maitland, explaining further that the older adults have a lot to accomplish, and the church is one of the few places where they can do it.[1]

We do know that most Americans declare a belief in God, and women have a higher attendance record of churchgoing at all ages than men.[2] But social gerontologists tell us that more specific behavior and meaning is difficult to measure. Moreover, much of what we know is based on limited and dated studies.

Most importantly, it appears that a distinction must be made between church attendance and private practice (attendance alone does not signify spirituality of the elder, since it can be heavily dependent on factors like physical disability or the demanding care of another). All in all, major disagreement continues as to whether persons, over time actually become more religious.[3]

By looking at private devotional practices, our original question of what has changed and what remains important becomes primary. It means looking at our own religious habits, aware that these times offer what Alan Jones calls a spiritual supermarket. What is best for all? If it is known that the elder's devotional life at home increases,[4] i.e., reading the Bible, prayer, viewing media presentations, do we support this trend with our time and effort? Do we teach about prayer? Do we provide quality programs for video viewing? Placing positive value on meditative practices is an unpopular stance for us, and brings to the fore our own conflicts.

With society's current emphasis on the active, instant, and loudly-voiced, we often choose not to relate to the elder at this level. Though the church throughout history gave us direct and personal recorded witness of individuals who, at every age, found incredible meaning in the private practice of devotion, many of us in the church today tend to renounce its value.

But note it is not the aged alone who are finding valued meaning in private, interior searching. Consider the current enthusiastic response of many mid-life adults to contemplative writers such as Henry Nouwen, Thomas Merton and Richard Foster. Fortunately, we are seeing today how eastern forms of meditation have aided in removing negative cultural attitudes regarding inner awareness, practicing reflection, and prayerful Christian meditation.

We also may be under the false impression that the contemplative mode is open only to the monk or saint, as was once believed. But don't we all need regular spiritual disciplines that keep us turning to God? So what blocks the elder may be what blocks the rest of us. Older European methods of devotion, such as *An Introduction to the Devout Life,* suggest that devotional practice was once encouraged. There is also evidence[5] that devotional material was readily available in early America. Today, how many of us recall a parent's well-marked Bible, yet did not invite open discussion of what was being read? While the availability of the early devotional literature was tied to literacy and the invention of the printing press, it was also related to such issues as preserving the faith and doctrines of the church! Some would say the early metaphors used no longer apply. As Carol Ochs argues, the journey metaphor suggests that God is found only at the end of our lives, denying God's presence in earlier times and ages. Though the value of tradition is imbedded in all of us, we know it is not lack of personal funds or ability to read that interferes with daily religious focus or habit. But if metaphors of stairs or ladders, or the *Exercises* of Ignatius or the *Treatises* of Eckhart do seem outmoded, where are other forms, where are the spiritual giants writing contemporary equivalents? By turning inward, perhaps the elders are indirectly asking the church to do what it finds difficult in doing, that is, identifying, practicing and leading us into more meaningful appropriate forms of basic spirituality. On the other hand, do we have strong demands for more devotional literature? Or, docs the elder need to speak to us and share with us a deepened level of communion with God that has been discovered during a long life? Are *they* the giants, thwarted by custom, culture, and forced anonymity?

Of course, moving away from standardized practices can be frightening. But the church in America has the opportunity to dialogue with the elder. What we assume is already known on both sides may not be so, while a state of readiness for more instruction may exist. It is up to the leadership to become tuned in to individuals who are teetering on age/faith fences.

The diversity of the age group is obvious here. While some may welcome aids to devotion learned from the past, others will be open to new or additional avenues. Rigid patterns discarded as meaningless may need to be replaced by new forms, perhaps based on updated scholarship, interpretation, or social acceptance. The contrast with other age groups is also obvious. Though the younger parishioner may have tried yoga, the older adult may not be familiar with helpful fundamental procedures such as finding a quiet, special private place, or deliberately choosing and saving a particular time of day for any practice of prayer. While these behavior patterns are not new to the devout, they may seem strange to a person raised in a togetherness culture. Likewise, while the retreat experience for a youth may feel like imposition from the outside, to the mature adult Christian the desire for quiet time with God grows from within. The willingness is chosen.

The elder today is more likely to be familiar with discipline as a necessary tool, and may welcome more information about technical methods or processes, such as centering prayer, chanting, journaling, and individual/group Bible study. Of these, journaling may hold special meaning (many resources are available). This may have strong appeal to a generation familiar with frequent letter writing and diary keeping, making this a task with recognizable value.

Sometimes words get in our way of interpreting what is really happening to the person of mature faith. It may be a case of updating words like "detachment" and "contemplative," into contemporary meaning and usage.

Any metaphor about emptying or stripping away may seem too 16th century to us, but the elder today recognizes meaning here. Many will have found from their own experience that they have freely chosen to discard what is superfluous. The attraction today to the life and words of St. Teresa of Avila can be found in: "He who has God finds he lacks nothing. God alone suffices." Long-winded is not what cousin Mabel seeks. Pestering with the irrelevant is not desired. She already knows what cuts through petty and false, to the peace where new energy is miraculously provided.

Most of all, the elder may be in a good place for listening. The aged pastor, priest, or nun, in particular, may have established regular patterns of devotions, but may be thirsty to both express glorious experiences or hear about new insights found by others in prayer. Endless afternoons and evenings can be transformed into sharing what has been heard and learned from lives tuned faithfully to the will of God.

The mystic elder who wants only God, who is seeking union with God, is in a different place from the one just learning that prayer is more than asking or sitting still. For the latter, the being open, the gratitude, the letting go, the praising, may need to be taught or supported.

Some find the prayers of others are the best starting places for their own. The Serenity Prayer, attributed to Reinhold Niebuhr, may be helpful. Others will rebel at this, saying aging is anything but serene, wanting the passionate state verified. For others, excerpts from famous spiritual leaders, grouped according to the reader's personality type, may be helpful.[6] Then again, brief biographies of known figures, or sayings of the desert fathers can be inspirational. It is not implied here that an active prayer life is easy or painless. Aging is an aerobic stage of spiritual bending and stretching.

Centering prayer, for example, is a technique that can be difficult to master without guidance, and time to read the holy scriptures does not mean ease in doing so. Bible reading, though once primarily a Protestant way of devotion, may now be available to everyone, but reading of a particular passage may need to be accompanied by suggestions on how to do so, such as, awareness that individual words can be savored; that original contexts can need examination. Or, questions may arise...Is there a message here for a lonely person like myself? asks aged Clara...Can I compare my spiritual journey to this biblical one?

For those elders who want another approach, there is now a wide range of possible periodical aids. For example, The United Methodist Church publishes a quarterly large-print, full-color magazine, *Mature Years,* which includes meditations for each day with an in-depth weekly commentary. Devotional bimonthly magazines from *The Upper Room* include one in large print and one for Spanish speaking congregations. Clergy will find the loose-leaf notebook, *The Prayer Services for the Elderly,* published by the Archdiocese of Kansas City helpful in small groups.

The church must also be alert to issues such as lack of privacy and fear of ridicule within the desire for devotional life. Reliance on God is not a generally talked about thing. The grey-haired woman next door may willingly talk about the altar cloth she lovingly embroidered last year, but she may choose not to discuss her personal practices. It would be more helpful if she could. The known major role of the widow in the early church was an active participation in regular prayer meetings.[7]

The elder has begun a new kind of inner attention. This may include a glad relief from external forces that seem dictatorial, or a pleasurable remembering that includes looking at what has not been heretofore carefully examined. This process has been generally attributed to psychiatrist Robert Butler who termed it "life-review." Thought to be brought on by awareness of finitude, this process happens spontaneously and is considered a normal developmental phase. It does raise the question of possible excessive psychic pain on top of disability, loss, and financial insecurity. Christians, in such review, can seek in prayer the forgiveness that makes new life possible. What *is* known is that the reorganizing of life's meaning, preceding death, can be a positive step to the elder.

Florida Scott-Maxwell, famed author and analytical psychologist, clarifies the value of life-review for her, and shares a common attitude toward death. At 82 she kept a private notebook that was eventually published successfully as *The Measure of My Days*.

> You need only claim the events of your life to make yourself yours. When you truly possess all you have been and done, which may take some time, you are fierce with reality. When at last age has assembled you together, will it not be easy to let it all go, lived, balanced, over?[8]

She also shared a common attitude toward death in her writings. Contrary to popular belief, fear of death is not a major concern.[9] This seems to be in contrast to medieval times when a lingering death was preferred, allowing time to make oneself right with God.

In our observation of the religious life of the older adult we must not undervalue congregational worship as meaningful. Any guidance in private practice—to avoid excessive individualism or spiritualism—includes reference to some form of communal worship when possible. To be able to partake of the sacrament, a Christian symbol of remembrance, is important. In addition, and in contrast to solitary life-review, remembering can take the form of story sharing. According to one church leader[10] who has developed some meaningful church-school lessons around reminiscence, remembering *with others* aids faith process in community.

Dosia Carlson, ordained executive director of the Beatitudes Center for Developing Older Adult Resources in Arizona, reminds us of the adaptations easily made in our sanctuaries to enhance the quality of corporate worship for all.[11]

Hearing and sight changes require devices, including adequate public address systems and large print words in programs and music. She also reminds us of the comfort derived from engaging in familiar elements of rituals.

As to specific religious images, what can be included and interpreted in a helpful manner for the elder member? Evelyn Whitehead suggests six as starters:

1. Personal salvation: one's values/achievements will endure in the continuing life of God.
2. Hope: confidence that one's life is part of God's plan.
3. A religious sense of time and personal history.
4. God's unconditional love; not based on works.
5. Spiritual discipline of letting go of false distractions.
6. Image of Christians as pilgrim-on-the-way.[12]

Being "on the way" surely may suggest individual help. Knowing the elder is already on that sometimes painful interior journey, it may be time to reconsider the once accepted practice of seeking spiritual direction. There is, if we can admit it, an attraction to the hope of finding one spiritually-oriented person who can walk with us—dare to accompany us—as we find the courage to question, affirm, or reaffirm our faith!

The clergy here can become scapegoats. The inability of any pastor to enter into a conversational relationship of a spiritual nature may reflect a void that is hard to face. Is it too much to ask clergy to go back to prioritizing spiritual basics? An elder will be led only by the astute person able to latch on to that vague but recognizable "knowing" of the heart.

One-to-one relationships teach us, and yet they are often avoided. Though a trained pastoral counselor can support an effort of evoking memory with specific techniques, sometimes it is the layperson who is available or present to walk through painful recollection with another, aiding in the resolving of unacknowledged conflict. What is being asked of us is to remember that while we may be stuck, standing in a store deciding which toothpaste brand to select, our elder friend may be caught up in determining a weightier issue such as the knowledge of the forgiveness of God...or being loved in spite of what went before...or being assured, after confession, that reconciliation can be reached. Let's predict that the counterpart of the once popular, *Hello God, Its Me, Margaret,* will someday reach the bookshelves. This will be a book about an elder, not a child, who addresses God, revealing openly his or her innermost puzzlements and perspectives. Yet we know the beloved Psalms already do this. They are the only part of the Bible that are a person's word to God rather than God's word made known to us...Is this why we love them so? why we incorporate them into our most personal occasion of worship? why we breathe them into our being when we joyfully come together, when we rejoice in the life of someone no longer with us? Note their continued pertinence to generation after generation. Surviving countless copyings, printings in strange languages, updated translations, and packed with pain and praise and plea, inspiring and lifting, they still speak to individual and corporate experience of sickness, defeat, disillusionment, poverty of spirit...leading to new heights of joy and fulfillment.

One thing remains unchanged. Any change in process within our personal or corporate prayer life remains secondary to motivation. Only the courageous church will be able to embark on the new and unfamiliar, or the already proven but revitalized kinds of devotional practice.

Suggested Reading:

Beginning to Pray In Old Age, Susan Coupland

Aging As A Spiritual Journey, Eugene Bianchi

Exploring Spiritual Direction: An Essay on Christian Friendship, Alan Jones

Video: *A Still, Small Voice*

Church Resource #7: Useful Bible References

Brevity of human life	Psalm 90:12
Pastoral attitude toward elders	I Timothy 5:1,2
Perspective of elder is God as merciful	Psalm 37:25
Commandment to honor parents	Exodus 20:12
Intergenerational affection	Ruth 1:1–18
Elder female as model of holiness	Luke 2:36–38
Fear of aging	Psalm 71:9
Caring as presence not words	Job 2:13
Attractiveness of wisdom in aged	Sirach 25:4–6
Aged leader shows good sense	2 Samuel 19:34–37
Elder role on deathbed ensures tradition	Genesis 47:29–49:33
Widow's mite of great significance	Luke 21:1–4
God's identification with helpless	Exodus 22:21–23
A man of 85 brags of strength	Joshua 14:10–11
Abuse of elder sign of decadence	Isaiah 47:6

8

RETHINKING WISDOM
AND MATURITY

Two words are examples of misunderstanding. Recently, a TV talk-show host, on learning the guest had reached the age of 54, demands tips about wisdom for the viewing audience. In the mind of the host, the logical sequence of thought appears to be that older equals automatic advice to share. A teen-age girl tells her young date for the evening that his actions are immature. In the mind of the girl certain behavior defies convention.

These words, "wisdom" and "maturity," are tied to our view of aging. Is this accurate? Are they embedded, fairly, into our unexamined knowing? Since they tend to be the common points at which we embark on church programming, and because positive qualities associated with advanced age need to be lifted up and clearly identified, let's take a closer look. Wisdom and maturity are generally linked. What can we learn of such generalizations from our use and disuse?

The words suggest a broad, cross-cultural understanding. WISDOM—"Conventional wisdom is international, although each locale gives it its own peculiar qualities."[1] MATURITY— "Maturity is fundamentally a social idea, and it differs from place to place and era to era."[2] Thus both words are of such broad usage that we will try to narrow our thinking.

Too often wisdom is a blanket expression that covers much

we never seriously appraise, both repelling and attracting. Pictures in books of bearded faces, or characters in other cultures cloud our knowing. Tellers of stories, hermits in seclusion, erudite figures in long robes subtly tease us. Reality or illusion? First cousin to knowledge or unattainable elevation?

Too often maturation is defined as biological development only. This suggests a peak period followed by decline. In truth, there are many kinds of maturity, and we are concerned here with moving away from a scientific definition to the maturation of our faith. This, too, in turn, implies growth and the option of being increasingly transformed to the likeness of God's son (Romans 8:29).

Wisdom appears to come from others, but how and in what form? Though quick to say she or he has it, does it come by story, anecdote, attitude, action, parable, person, or possibly by intuitive conclusion?

Professor David Maitland reminds us of two erroneous attitudes: a) that only elderly may become wise, and b) that all elderly will do so.[3] This rings true to our experience as we recall both the youth in our acquaintance who were wise for their chronological age, and the elders we have known who by habit, behavior or life-style, would never qualify by our not easily definable standards.

Looking first at religious viewpoints, we westerners generally associate wisdom with biblical knowledge. We lift out or like to randomly quote such favorites as Job 12:12 "Wisdom is with the ages," and Psalm 90:12, "Teach us to number our days that we may apply our hearts to wisdom." The latter appears to be a plea to God that we recognize. It is about being aware that time on earth is limited and help is needed if we are to concentrate on godly things.

According to Old Testament scholars, wisdom within Israel can broadly mean a whole body of literature which has a teaching function. (Consider the book of Proverbs.) This thus came out of a group-oriented, kinship, community context. It implies life experience and the desire to know what is needed.[4] It also implies that wisdom is something that is acquired through effort.[5] Rewards or prosperity go to those who practice certain instruction from God.[6]

The so-called Wisdom books of the Bible are Proverbs, Job, Ecclesiastes, and Sirach and the Wisdom of Solomon within the Apocrypha. Davidson calls these "the Cinderella in the household of faith."[7] By this he meant that until at least the post-exilic period of Israel's history their value was secondary.

According to New Testament scholars, true wisdom is found only in the person of Jesus Christ (1 Corinthians 2:3). This introduces a new concept of wisdom as a gift rather than something earned by certain behavior according to Jewish law.

Most commonly, we speak of wisdom and old age simultaneously. But Job is the most powerful story to negate this idea when we consider his directing the friends to its real source, God.[8] The force of this story continues to entice and repel our understanding.

So what observations from scripture seem assured? First, there seems to be a clear distinction between worldly wisdom versus heavenly wisdom (consider I Corinthians 18:25 and James 3:17 "But wisdom from above is first pure, then peaceable, gentle, willing to yield, full of mercy and good fruits, without a trace of partiality or hypocrisy"). It is also separate from knowledge, but often paired with it. (Consider Colossians 2:2,3.)

Secondly, according to Psalm 90:2, the wise man uses his limited time on earth to develop a mind of wisdom. It doesn't happen easily or automatically. Moreover, it is a new kind of learning by which the heart is made wise.[9] Not an intellectual process, it can be available to everyone!

Lastly, wisdom is associated with choosing God. The fear of the Lord can be the beginning place. (Consider Deuteronomy 30:19, 20, Proverbs 9:10 and Psalm 111:10). The implication of both the Old and the New Testaments is that with increased awareness we, as well as the aged, can become wiser by developing this relationship with God. We can agree with an educator[10] that our faith will become mature as we struggle to understand what God wants. While we may cry out for specific words to define the qualities of being wise, the ability "to see" may be the aspect of "knowing" that transcends any trivial quest.

Accustomed to only traditional ways of authority, the intuitive way of knowing is less familiar to youth but what elders are more apt to trust. This heightened awareness can include the humorous, "Your knees buckle but your belt won't," of the anonymous senior, to a serious search for one's own appropriate response to a catastrophe.

To add to our confusion in the 20th century, a variety of other explanations are volunteered: "Wisdom comes from giving thanks";[11] it "begins in self-loathing";[12] it comes from life experience, "well-digested";[13] not to mention the wealth of scholarship connecting it with the feminine.

Apparently the wise and mature person of any age examines his or her life choices, seeking wisdom in prayer and deeper relationships. The term "spiritual formation" is gaining in popularity today. Spiritual maturity involves necessary growth through education and striving.

There will always be those of us who associate wisdom with perfection. (Consider 1 Peter 5:10.) Will this not create an additional burden of unfair expectation on those already burdened by marginalization, loss, or physical decline? Even Carl Jung had trouble accepting the role in old age.[14] Yet a church historian reminds us that while modern usage implies that there is no room for improvement, ancient Christian writers intended a more helpful "continual movement into God's love."[15]

Are we asking for renewed understanding of old roles? Are we asking for recognition of subtle things we all are trying to learn that are not the product of a college degree? Consider what Duane Ewers has given us in his basic dimension of a mature faith:

1) a person of mature faith trusts and believes in God.
2) a person of mature faith experiences the fruits of faith described in Scripture.

3) a person of mature faith integrates faith with life.
4) a person of mature faith seeks spiritual growth.
5) a person of mature faith experiences and nurtures faith in the community of faith.
6) a person of mature faith holds life-affirming values.
7) a person of mature faith advocates social change.
8) a person of mature faith acts and serves.[16]

Moreover, when anyone—the older adult in particular—has the gift or mature fruits of the spirit to contribute (consider Galatians 5:22, 33 as to love, joy, patience, kindness, gentleness, faithfulness, self-control) how, when, where, and under what circumstances can this be done? Our culture defies it. Caught up in what has been defined as an information society with the bits and pieces of trivial factual stuff mechanically recorded-stored-written down, we exclude reference to the kinds of knowledge and truth that also could be passed on, picked up, learned or transmitted in a more personal way.

To feel one has either of the following could be incredibly painful: 1) nothing of worth to share, or 2) bundles of intangible truth, universal in nature, that could enable the next generation to live more fully. A leader of women's retreats devotes one chapter of her guidebook[17] to encouraging the older woman to share wisdom she was unaware she represented! And a touching poem by elder Lilly Palace entitled "Crazy Wisdom"[18] points to what has been learned that others overlook, i.e., appreciation of small things. A surprising revelation of the same concept is seen in Proverbs 30:24–28.

The wisdom of God is not always identified by so-called important cultural standards, but can be experienced firsthand, or made known to us in our reflective and awaiting stance.

> ...any mature person looking back on their own past life, will be forced to recognize factors in that life which cannot be attributed to heredity, environment,

opportunity, personal initiative or mere chance. The contact which proved decisive, the path unexpectedly opened, the other path closed, the things we felt compelled to say, the letter we felt compelled to write. It is as if a hidden directive power, personal, living, free, were working through circumstance and often against our intention or desire; pressing us in a certain direction, and molding us to a certain design.[19]

Only the older adult has the capacity for the long view and the message therein, while the church is the one place where individual intuitive experience can be appreciated and shared, and a context is given in which the meaning may be framed. The Holy Spirit empowers each one of us.

The church is the place where each member, regardless of age, is not only accepted but valued for skills, understanding, and experienced knowing. Daniel Jenkin's excellent chapter on the mature church[20] contributes to our understanding of a continuing growth process enriched by the diversity of gifts and the cooperative effort of those who worship together before scattering to do God's work in the world.

His analogy to the common understanding of the word "maturation" suggests observing whether growth is healthy. By this he means, is there feeding of the soil, watering, removal of weeds, along with the pruning and grafting? Patience is highlighted as the key to all kinds of gardening. In his words, the definition of maturity is concerned with freedom, choice, limitation, responsibility, and accountability. Applicable here is the statement that maybe the "greatest spiritual growth occurs as one struggles with physical loss and dying."[21]

In reference to the famous Bergman movie *Wild Strawberries*, in which the key figure, Dr. Borg, reaches old age, the author refers to the "state of having matured both in height and in stature, and of having reached the stage of one who now nourishes what he bears and produces."[22]

In a world that tends to equate maturity with well-dressed and socially acceptable behavior, we have more redefining to do. We in the church could be more open, individually, to concepts shared by such people as the Whiteheads. As Christian scholars, they define Christian maturity as a "seasoning of instincts,"[23] meaning that it is in the family and the parish, through many seasons, that we are influenced by appropriate amounts of positive feelings and values.

Waiting for studies to show, or surveys to yield, denies our intuitive knowing and sharing of what is valuable. Always in process, a not-knowing remains, and a knowing propels forward. Wisdom is not something, but it is Someone,[24] found and available in relationships and prayer.

The words "wisdom" and "mature" may defy easy definition today, but a path ahead is clear. Both relate us to God. Both relate us to others, whether they be bearded or babies. Most of all "we are called to a maturity and transformation beyond our own ability to change ourselves."[25]

"Yet among the mature we do speak wisdom, though it is not a wisdom of this age or of the rulers of this age, who are doomed to perish. But we speak God's wisdom, secret and hidden, which God decreed before the ages for our glory" (1 Corinthians 2:6-7).

Suggested Reading:

Women's Ways of Knowing, Mary Belenky

In the Ever After: Fairy Tales and the Second Half of Life, Allan Chinen

How Faith Matures, C. Ellis Nelson

Spiritual Maturity in the Later Years, James Seeber

Church Resource #8: Other Words that Call for New Understanding or Exploration

conservatorship	pilgrimage
ageism	senescence
sedentary life-style	validity
crystallized intelligence	life-review
paternalizes	despair
interiority	longevity
catastrophic illness	self-esteem
disengagement theory	contemplative
rites of passage	living will
senior olympics	chemotherapy
grief work	intervention
supplemental security income	senile dementia
life expectancy	gerontology

9

SPOTLIGHTING PLACE AND RELATIONSHIP

No adjustment is more difficult to the older adult than moving to a new place of residence where new persons and unaccustomed space become home. The stress on striking out on one's own when young to become self-supporting and independent does not coincide with cultural late-life messages to the older adult. Issues of privacy, independent living, companionship, and dignity are suddenly squelched or forgotten. They no longer apply.

Most important in the housing issue is the reminder that our concern must not center only on the old-old. There are millions who, after retirement, seek ways to remain independent as they simply scale down or reduce or change their living space. With the general shortage and high cost of decent shelter for all, with the changes in our building trades, the need will become intensified. Cost, shortage, and size of shelter is important to all adults.

At mid-life, factors concerning future housing escalate in importance. Where shall I go?...What size place do I really need?...Once my children are grown and off, why should I maintain extra space?...Who will take out the trash, paint and paper, shovel the snow?...Will real estate taxes continue to skyrocket?...Where are my friends choosing to live?...Will I be a bag lady, cold, out on the streets?

Perhaps what frightens most is the letting go; the giving up of the familiar—the neighborhood and the items associated with cherished moments. Specifically, the reduction of space is often related to loss of friends or spouse. Or, it can be the bulging photo albums, the comfortable chair by the window with the view. But more than furniture and knick-knack is the attachment to memories.

It was once strongly believed that because elders are less active and less involved, withdrawal (disengagement) was a natural part of aging. It was considered mutually agreeable that they be out of town and out of sight. Though this once popular theory is still debated, for those not restricted by physical or practical problems, active involvement in voluntary organizations, especially the church, is often their choice. This means that the proximity of the apartment to gathering places is still important.[1] Opportunities to maintain solid personal relationships in town, church, and neighborhood, meaning, to be able to give as well as receive, is as important to the elder as the location, size, and condition of the living space.

Stashed out of sight is not OK. When we subtly support the cultural practice of approving the elder as out of sight before considering alternatives, we are not only insensitive, but we make the situation even more crucial for our churches, our children, and grandchildren. If the elder is not part of everyday life, younger generations may never become accustomed to the ways and contributions of elders.

Emotional, as well as financial uncertainty crowd the mind of the person knowing some sort of move is immanent. We in the church must remember psychological needs are closely related to physical needs. If procrastination, or minor crisis, is present, or sympathetic personal help is lacking, wrong and hurried choices may result. Within a culture loaded with materialistic props and often spiritual neglect, the removal of the familiar can seem like death. While some may find a simpler life-style appealing, or a blessing, the stripping away of excess or consumer goods may to others feel like unbearable deprivation.

It is so important that the older adult feel part of every decision made, especially as to place. This means to be consulted and included in both medical and family-related issues. Because the body slows down does not mean the individual does not have clear and definite suggestions or preferences. The appeal of mild winters may be foremost in Uncle Jasper's mind; or, for Aunt Janice, the simple addition of hand rails or widened doorways can mean remaining in her present location. Minor changes can often be the best answers.

Hopefully, new options as to housing, along with new technology, will appear on our horizons. For now, there is a limited variety from which to choose. Smaller apartments or condos may be easily accommodated. Then again, equity from a home sold can assure a wide selection while at the same time a middle-income renter may be pushed out by condo conversions.

Other specific options as to area, according to Ken Dychtwald, can be considered. These are the recreation-centered retirement communities like Sun City[2] or, for the educated, increasingly popular, are the college towns such as Ann Arbor, Michigan; Burlington, Vermont; and Winston Salem, North Carolina.[3] These boast amenities of library, concert and other cultural events and activities.

A popular temporary type of housing, just catching on, is the Echo concept. Recently brought to the U.S. from Australia, these "granny flats" are small, self-contained units. They can be put up on the property of an adult relative (assuming there are no zoning restrictions), and are removable. Advocates claim they are more economical than remodeling a private home for an inside apartment. Cost is approximately $20,000.[4] While elders may have been taught that one-fourth of the income is adequate for housing, many are paying a great deal more. So, at the other end of the spectrum, and with our economic recession, there are increasing numbers of elderly without shelter. Some are trying home sharing.[5] Low income housing, partially financed by HUD, can mean reduced rents. But these are often shunned as demeaning.

For the elder seeking permanent, assisted living of some sort, all options need to be investigated, described, and thoroughly understood. Often owned and maintained by a religious denomination, community, private or fraternal organization, the quality of care and service varies. The difference between intermediate and skilled medical care needs to be clarified. Lengthy convalescence, need for medical supervision, etc., influence choices.

To move to a skilled nursing home environment can, of course, be traumatic. The elder regards it with fear and hostility.[6] This may follow hospitalization or be dictated as a necessity because of confusion, chronic illness, mobility problems, etc. The nursing home, for those needing full-time nursing skills, can be first rate, and all do not deserve negative media attention.

Many books on the choice of levels of care are now on the market and can be extremely helpful. Suggested questions to ask or test out (such as the attitudes of the staff, the licensing, the assured access of residents to doctors' care) are helpfully formulated. Informal, advance conversations with residents as well as staff are usually recommended.

The buckling down on standards of care by government regulation in recent years does not assure personalized, loving care. The resident who said to his visitor, "I'm buried alive," could mean, a) painful truth as to inadequate care, or b) a mental condition that needs attention. Every state has a written document of the rights of its nursing home residents, and any problems experienced can be reported to the Nursing Home Ombudsman. This is a representative of your local Office On Aging.

Life care is an option for those financially able. Early choice ensures not only shelter and services but the added plus of intensive medical care later when needed. The number of these jumped from 100 in 1979 to 800 in 1988.[7] Entrance fees at a place like the Collington Episcopal Life Care Community in Maryland range from $30–500,000, with monthly payments of $500–2000.[8] Such high cost in itself, available to the few, should trouble the Christian conscience.

One of the disadvantages of any facility can be the distance from mainstream living. In the foothills or downtown metropolis, feeling forgotten, unimportant, and isolated can breed depression, loneliness and despair. It is imperative that any church understand the triad of solitude, loneliness and isolation. Solitude that invites an opportunity for spiritual development is not the same as physical and emotional isolation. The church must find ways to help elders stuck in institutions to remain connected with the community and with God. It is good news that our cities and towns are moving toward better community services for the aged. Thus, it means that those, who so choose, can remain in their homes for a longer period.

What becomes increasingly apparent within the housing issues is the naming of persons who will be involved in the decision making and the caregiving at all levels. As we know, the family itself has gone through considerable change in recent years. Consider, "...when we gather around the table we give new meaning to the word 'family' because we are the latest word in relatives, an amalgam of his-and-her children, somebody's niece, an occasional nephew, a wandering friend, and at least two leftover uncles and aunts. ('Are they yours, his, or hers?')"[9] Even books are available for children about distinguishing different kinds of family.[10] The conflicts of need, the restriction of space, and the lack of funds can create pressure on decisions to be made involving those who love and provide for each other.

This does not include the fact that there are many aged without any next of kin, many having outlived spouse, children and early associates. It is a myth, however, that elders in adult societies are abandoned by their families. Though not in the same household, most live near a relative or child.[11]

However, all family relationships vary and can be emotionally loaded. The old adage "love me, love my dog" may change to the new adage of "love me, love my mother and grandmother who also live with me." While most families do their best, care involving round-the-clock attention in the home can be a terrible strain. Though shared responsibilities and respect can be practiced in earlier stages, later problems and frustrations influence all concerned.

Questions can remain unsaid, simmering. Questions latent with anxiety, such as: "What do I really owe my parents?" or, "I don't want to live alone, but my daughter doesn't want me!" Guilt, rivalry, manipulation, etc.—any unresolved patterns—can exude or disrupt honest attempts at caregiving. (See chapter 13 for additional comments on caregiving.)

Sometimes it is peer friends who have a big part in the decision making. Surprisingly, this happens more often than family members are aware of. (Consider the common pre-death confiding, as in the man who told, not his son, but his golf buddy of those intermittent chest pains.) The significant other may not be what any of us expect.

It is here that the church might take note, with the word "friendship" holding new meaning. Though the value of friendship, old or new, in aging is often included in older gerontological literature,[12] a fine new article by Rebecca Adams can update us.[13] Though the elder has lost many of his or her friends from youth or early employment association, the friendship label now has wider connotations. It can include anyone not kin or not a coworker. Moreover, to declare friendship may be the only voluntary thing that remains. To have friends engenders psychological well-being because, 1) peer implies commonality, 2) it is not an obligatory relationship, and 3) it involves the person in the larger society not just within the family. Could it imply fun or temporary relief from worry and care? This, in turn, brings up the key issue of intimacy and its important place in the life of the elder.

We tend to view any closeness or sign of affection between elders as obscene or unnatural. But isn't it essential for persons of any age to love and feel loved? Intimacy can take many forms of expression, i.e., touching, belonging, trusting, and understanding; and it may be experienced simply through eye contact or movement.[14] Sexual activity declines, but it can continue to be a normal and satisfactory part of life, depending on psychological and social factors such as health of partner, or availability.[15] By building opportunity for quality relationships, the church can make a contribution to basic needs of the elder. By providing opportunities for friendship and trust to develop, the congregation ensures meaningful experiences that may prove supportive and primary in later years.

The author of **Sister Age** blames housing as the reason for the lonely elder "not staying sweet" today, and foresees trouble in the future as to both space and relationship:

> Our housing is to blame. It is said that by the end of this century most citizens in the Western world will have adapted themselves to living as family units in allotted spaces no bigger than a compact car. There will be at least four people to each cubicle; two parents, and...two children.

> ...There will be well-designed patterns for our prospective quarters, at least for sleeping, and hygiene will perforce be almost as necessary as oxygen, to avoid epidemics of everything from disease to civil mayhem.

> ...Day schools will take care of the children almost from birth. But what about lovemaking, and such prerequisites to procreation as a bit of privacy? Will that,

too, be scheduled, by the hour or two, in appointed governmental love-nests?[16]

The church can both change its attitude and heed the frank speculation. For a start, it can build up more practical communication networks.

For example, it can advertise or list in its newsletter known available housing in reliable neighborhoods. It can offer names and addresses of youth groups able to do yard work or jobs related to moving. It can sponsor a housing workshop that includes information about local facilities, and perhaps offer professional help to those who need accounting or paperwork done, thus assuring an elder's staying in his own place. It can develop a handyman program of skilled volunteers to do smaller maintenance jobs. It can design and carry out special celebratory services, such as the blessing of a new home.[17] This last ensures value and group participation in an event that is highly significant but often ignored.

Most of all, the church as loving advisor, practical friend, and moving consultant is not unrelated to the church as spiritual mentor.[18] Openness to all levels of relationship and need is our task, our ministry, our mission.

Unlike the young man from Ace Moving Co. who observed that the old lady had too many chairs and loudly said so, we can learn now to refrain from judgment while lovingly evaluating. (Might not the lady in question be fearfully hoping or expecting to have visitors to put in those empty chairs?) Or, when Grandpa arrives for a visit with a shoebox full of medical prescriptions, might not we tactfully refrain from sly, inappropriate comment, while at the same time suspecting and inquiring about overmedication?

The past record of forced and charitable institutionalization of the elderly—the poorhouse pauper, with all the confusion about the definition of senility, according to the then known medical theories[19]—as well as present trends, warn us to evaluate what we do and why we do it. Society's definitions change and do not necessarily reflect Christian motivation.

Today, we may find strong appeal in innovative housing ideas. Consider twelve adults sharing shelter, cooking, and space. For two dinners to prepare a month, there are twenty-two free evenings without kitchen duty.[20] *That* has merit. Or scattered site housing with its basic fee for delivery of services can have appeal.

Better yet, what about a new category of persons called by God to live *with* elders in their restricted, marginalized, compartmentalized, visually unpleasant space? With the Holy Spirit leading, we in the church can improvise new ways of expressing God's loving intent. Living longer need not mean unnecessary hardship.

In the future when we hear the phrase adequate and affordable we may find ourselves discarding cultural standards and applying instead Christian measures of generosity, provision for personal choice, and the presence of meaningful others.

Suggested Reading:

Elder Care: Choosing and Financing Long-Term Care, Joseph Matthews

When Love Gets Tough, Doug Manning

Church Resource #9: Make Church Family Tree
According to Residence or Relationship

man
woman
student
homeless
temporary
two friends
nursing home
grandparents
mother and son
widow and child
husband and wife
life-care facility
single older adult
congregate housing
father and daughter
retirees without kin
uncle aunt and nephews
grandparents and one child
bedridden frail older adult
husband and wife and one child
husband and wife and grandparent
mother and father and four children
intermediate medical care facility
grandparent divorced son grandchild
two married couples and three children
husband and wife and child and grandparent
recreation centered retirement community
CHURCH
CHURCH
CHURCH

10

FOCUSING ON
THE OLDER WOMAN

Grandmothers, widows, friends ...Image implies a popular visualization, and the abundance of older women is common knowledge. As images of women can be truthful or fictional, let's separate what we know from what we do not know. The fact that "survival of humanity depends on utilizing fully the energy of mature women"[1] makes it imperative.

The statistics reveal, first of all, that women live longer than men. For ages 65–69 there are 100 women for 83 men; after age 85 the ratio doubles or becomes 42 men for 100 women.[2] As of 1984 there were 10.4 million single women over 65.[3]

As the roles of all women expand, there *is* hope that the older woman will find or create *new* models that will affect us all. This will be necessary because the past and the present have not been easy for women of any age. The fictional literature of the American past, for example, with its varied emphases on seduction scenes, domestic melodramas, overt moralizing, victimized wives, isolation, and her portrayal in detective stories[4] is one way to indirectly document this. As she aged, she became the recipient of uncomplimentary nicknames of hag, witch, biddy, or shrew. These concentrated on negative body image, denying the positive contributions coming from mind and soul.

Children brought up on Victorian stories saw her portrayed as only an "other," outside community, an object existing only as plaything or teacher of proper behavior.[5] More recently, feminist Barbara Walker traced through history the changing image of elder woman from good crone, wise healer, to invisible, ugly crone.[6] Cultural definitions have dominated both a view of women in general and how a woman views herself.

Widow

The most familiar elder woman by category today is the widow. This is not surprising considering that there are now five times as many widows as widowers, and one-half of all women over 65 are just that.[7]

Again, keeping image in mind, let us view the status of the widow in the early church. According to scholar Jean Laporte, the church in scripture had a duty to help the many poor—a group that included the widow and orphan. They, in turn, were expected to hold exemplary roles as wise counselors and healers. Thus, there was a meaningful place for those living consecrated lives of prayer, continence and fasting. This role later declined during the rise of monasticism and the worship of virginity.[8] Today, if a role of the widow is defined at all, aside from being considered a threat, it is within psychological understanding of such issues as adaptation and level of education acquired within our culture.[9] Friends' testimonies as well as studies done, attest to all the negative imaging these many women experience. How can the church aid these persons in confronting the stereotype, and finding new meaning?

Grandmothers

Grandmother is currently enjoying a reinstatement of status. With increased longevity and the rising divorce rate, her role is rapidly expanding. Broad choices are often possible, and this may include parenting again to others' children. The rule, interpreted by one investigative team[10] is now "non-interference" in family matters. Grandma, too, is juggling her multiple roles that aging has brought her. She may take off for Tahiti, have a boyfriend, or just plain refuse to babysit. This comes at a time when experts are stating the importance of reclaiming the value of the close relationship between grandchildren and grandparents. Supposedly, Grams and Gramps have new roles as historian, mentor, role model, wizard and nurturer.[11] But are these new? Are they in actuality valued by society?

A recent claim based on cross-cultural research says that many cultures reflect a late life role reversal with the male becoming more contemplative and the woman more assertive.[12]

Single Female Adults

This group, perhaps more than others, reflects our ambivalence toward the older woman. While in our past there was both maiden lady and crotchety old maid, today many women have found dignity and meaning in choosing singleness. But this group, as we consider the most familiar categories, brings to mind the oft forgotten and major factor within our changing culture. That consideration is economics.

The largest and fastest growing group of persons living below the poverty level are unmarried. As of 1990, twenty-seven percent of women aged 65 and older who live alone are poor.[13] Add to this the growing awareness of those in minority status. Fifty-nine percent of minority older women over the age of 85 are poor.[14] Add to this the fact that black women over forty have always had the highest unemployment rate.[15] Then add to this the fact that women are the major caregivers to everyone...family, friend, spouse...and often wake up, too late, to the lack of funds and support needed in their own late life stages. For the women, the prime role as caregiver remains even when family structure fades. Who will be the caregiver for her?

The poor and marginalized older woman, regardless of race, has a difficult time. This is related to many factors, especially employment struggles in earlier years and the lack of the triad of adequate pension, Social Security rate, and savings. Women of all ages are paid seventy-two cents for every dollar men earn, and the gap widens with age.[16] We forget that the woman who was a homemaker most of her life is not eligible for her husband's benefits unless married for at least 20 years.

Where exactly does the church take part? Accepting truthful images, changing false ones, creating new ones is difficult but imperative. Aging is not a problem to be solved. It is lives to be lived. Taking the cultural definition of "poor, dumb, and ugly"[17] without appropriate response borders on the demonic. For starters, the elder must be recognized as someone who can do her own defining.

There was the persistent widow in Luke 18:1–8 who effected change in the system by pestering the judge relentlessly. Women's strengths have often included obstinacy and steadfastness in the face of adversity, and must continue to do so.

There are also those women who, influenced by cultural definition, choose, for example, cosmetic surgery to alter and assure their passive place in cultural expectations as long as possible. Others find relief in humor, hiding power within innovative approaches. *Be An Outrageous Older Woman a R*A*S*P,* a book by gerontologist Ruth Jacobs, designed for assertiveness, includes this element along with other advice.

Somehow, we must wake up to the fact that the changing social and religious roles are deeply affected by the economic scene. When it is publicized that the economic needs of women are often doubled in aging, will we lament the resulting lost contributions to God's world enough to take community action?

We know we will no longer be able to call older women nagging, passive, asexual. Those aging through the ranks of demographic groupings will refuse to accept some of those assigned roles. With the help of Christian guidelines, such as the program *Women of Vision:* Women Empowering and Visioning Effectively, developed by the Episcopal Church Women, taking charge will be more common. But attitudes toward women in general must change before images that are false will be discarded.

The current literature on aging and the older woman places emphasis on new beginnings, with special attention to valuing the body which in the past has brought so much cultural denigration. Facing crisis, independence, medical systems, career options and all the rest calls for intellectual choices involving all kinds of emotional and physical strength as well as communal support.

It is clear that data points to older women as expressing a stronger religious identification than men.[18] This has implications for the institutional church as the logical heart, hands, and voice with the oppressed. Yet the exact role of the church is unclear. Much of the work is already carried on by older women; all forms of worship and social events include many of those aunts, widows and grandmas. Sixteen thousand women are now clergy. As leaders, are they facilitating the necessary change? Are the economically privileged speaking out on behalf of the others?

"Many older women must learn both to request things for themselves and to deal with powerful bureaucracies."[19] Worn out and worn down from past cultural imaging and demands, will the older woman be able to see the challenge of her extended life span as a time of modeling or as a burden of extended suffering?

The six year old, on describing his bed-ridden loving Grandma, insisted "Grandma is here all of the time, but her body is shrinking...I mean, Grandma's body is getting smaller, but Grandma is not shrinking. Just her body."[20]

"And a little child shall lead them."[21]

Suggested Readings:

Survival of the Spirit, Ruth Gray

The World of the Older Woman, Gari Lesnoff-Caravaglia

Church Resource #10:
Situations for Small Group Discussion

Mrs. Wonderful sings in the choir, organizes suppers, leads Bible study, drives youth to retreats, and keeps trim with yoga, tennis, and cross-country skiing. How can the church aid her in preparation for a less active aging?

She has been homebound for 20 years. After a lifetime of active service in the church and community she wonders what she has done to deserve the isolation. To compensate she eats three donuts, two chocolate bars and a six pack of coke each day and sleeps a lot. Can the church have a part in changing her habits?

At church on Sunday morning Clare, aged 75, is so upset during morning worship by the noisy antics of baby Jessica that she angrily confronts the mother at the church door; tells her the disruptive child belongs in the nursery. The young mother breaks down and sobs but finds a way to lash out in return. Both adults exit angrily. The staff wants advice.

Mabel lost her husband last winter. She is 74. The week after the funeral church members and friends found thoughtful ways to express their concern, but within a year she suddenly realized she was being excluded from accustomed activities. What are the options for both her and the church?

You are a resident at Goldencare Retirement Facility at 26 Wildwood Drive. You are still active and like to make new friends. But what is most painful is the lack of opportunity for expressions of intimacy. The nurses snicker when any touching takes place; you know that sexuality is not welcome. In whom can you confide about your needs without being laughed at?

11

APPRAISING THE VALUE OF WORK AND LEISURE

Our views about work and free time are outdated. Retirement, in particular, has brought attention to this, signaling new dilemmas. Retirement can mean relief from a disliked job. It can mean visions of sun-filled days to do all those things that earlier life stages did not permit. Bob from middle-management at GE says he'll golf "till he drops"; Bernice with 42 years of secretarial service says she's going to travel, i.e., cruise, fly, run away to exotic places. It could also mean finding new values beyond learned expectation. But sometimes—and often first of all—realized dreams take on negative perspectives.

The elders of today were programmed that what one did for paid employment was what mattered most. The discovery that, 1) endless time to pursue certain activities seldom satisfies, or 2) learning too late that a former job gave identity, challenge and meaning, may come as a surprise. The once learned Protestant ethic[1] of effort, and the accumulation of material goods as evidence of God's blessing, may cease to apply.

When we learn that the suicide rate for American men in retirement is four times higher than in any other stage[2] it is time to evaluate. Stories such as *The Village Singer*[3] depicting the forced retirement of the church's leading soprano being responsible for her sudden death give evidence of strong cultural forces.

From the beginning of time human beings have needed to do some kind of work in order to survive. However, our ideas about the nature of work have changed from early biblical literal interpretation, through the concepts of the Reformation, and to modern day technological advances that supposedly made work easier and better. But somewhere along the way, when work changed from a form of individual responsibility to repetitious tasks according to someone else's time frame, its purpose was blurred. Most of today's elders who were employed, kept on relentlessly pushing the lever at the plant without feeling that an alternative or recourse was available. And what was born is evidenced in the current best-selling book, **Waiting For the Week-End.**[4] Two days free from that impersonal nine-to-five employment became a frantic time for what felt like varied forms of compensation. Now, in retirement, a longer time period provides the opportunity to do more of the same on a full-time basis! But what exactly *is* leisure?

From the perspective of too many days of so-called unemployment, time on one's hands does not appear to define leisure accurately.[5]

> ...20th century seems to demand half of life be disciplined, rational and productive while the other half be undisciplined, irrational and consumerist. Not surprisingly, some people get confused: they are lazy on the job or they labor at their free time...U.S. society appears...schizoid.[6]

Thus we see the two words—work and leisure—as locked into relation to each other. At the same time, many changes in our economic system are currently taking place in the workplace— from flextime to job sharing. Even our attitudes, too, seem to be changing, and we must find and define new values related to leisure and work for both the elder and ourselves. Seward Hiltner's early effort[7] to formulate a theology of aging included the need for a reconsideration of work and leisure.

As Gabriel Moran suggests, we can begin to untangle the meaning by drawing a distinction between job and work, and between leisure as free time and leisure as contemplation.[8] (Note: In chapter 7 we have already noted our cultural trouble with fitting the value of contemplation into our life-style and understanding.) A "job" suggests pay for services, and leisure is more than free time. Moreover, do we believe—as Pieper suggests—that "true leisure is possible only when man [sic] is at one with himself [sic]?"[9]

It is helpful for those of us caught in age-related dilemmas to recall a summation of Aristotle's understanding of leisure and pleasure.[10] Leisure was once thought to be an active, moral activity or capacity that, though only possible for some, provided time for contemplation for a particular group. This was thought to be of highest value. Add to this a later evaluation of leisure as celebration which was also related to worship.[11] Thus leisure, in its historic context, had strong ties with higher things. How we lost this may not be as important as whether or not we want to retrieve it.

As we reconsider leisure, we need also to replace our attitudes about work "with a holistic approach to life that does not diminish the truly personal, community, and societal value of work, but makes both life and work qualitatively different by complementing work with leisure."[12]

For the elder, there can be new satisfaction in new tasks while viewing work and leisure together. Opportunities for self-expression, part-time employment, second careers, commitments out of choice, etc., should make the transition into retirement years less traumatic. Changing cultural factors such as increased time for developing avocations,[13] affluence, and the "new inconsistencies in what is considered age-appropriate behavior"[14] should also make future transitions easier.

"To confuse us, leisure can now mean recreation, education, volunteerism *and* work!"[15] Perhaps most importantly, without pressure to achieve, there can be what we call "quality time," the opportunity for taking time to be fully with others which in itself has value as an "ego transcending quality."[16]

Reminders that we are saved by God's grace, not by the job we had or have, can lift up all of us to a better view of self, others, and world. "Leisure is a time, a place, a circumstance, an opportunity, a method and a desire to gain perspective on life and what it is all about. Who has any greater responsibility than the church to help this happen?"[17]

But how can the church do this? First, we can encourage quiet, reflective time, teach spiritual disciplines and elevate worship experiences. Second, we cannot pretend that the lives of members function as they once did. "No longer can the church depend on an established routine in the lives of its parishioners."[18] Third, we can identify what we can do in the way of programming geared to early retirement. We can reeducate or prepare the individual for changes in the workplace and in self-expectations. We could start with classes about both finding meaning in, and understanding the concept of, vocation.

For example, the realization that work is best interpreted as a vocation, a calling, a summoning[19]...as from God...can be helpful. It can even be viewed "as a lifelong conversation with God."[20] Then we can move from finding meaning only in what we do, to finding meaning in who we are. According to Viktor Frankl, who wrote extensively on the subject, the search for meaning is the fundamental drive for all of us. According to Melvin Kimble,[21] this is the particular crisis of old age. T.S. Eliot in *Four Quartets* reminds us that looking back "we had experience but missed the meaning."[22] The past has value that can be reclaimed, reinterpreted. Time to study the landscape from the porch of life, and reflect thereon, can mean good things for our churches. The movement away from achievement toward spiritual dimensions can lead to self-worth, which in turn leads to "how can I act out my faith?"

There are tasks in the church of every kind that must be done. Issues requiring experience and problem solving need to be attacked. At the same time, elders in early retirement are experiencing momentary confusion as to their worth, waiting to be included and useful. Life has taught them about the value of meaningful work. Likewise, published facts about the positive work habits of the elder, that include dependability, minimal absenteeism, etc., are repeatedly recorded.[23] So let's get the people and the jobs together! Being practical can be a beginning.

We will have to give up our own outdated concepts of leisure and work habits. See the elders as a special group legitimately engaged in creative leisure. Swallow adages about idleness being the devil's workshop. Exhaustingly busy ourselves, can we forget ourselves long enough to value another's contribution? It may mean a new level of learning and selflessness that deepens our understanding of Christ's work and our own. As the church we can help change negative ideas about work, to positive ones about living purposefully, by drawing an analogy that supports our Christian heritage.

Retirement has been likened to a space capsule atop a booster rocket. "The first stage...our working lives...is...left to fall away while the second stage, though small, is free to change directions, turn...move...change orbits...perform actions that were impossible before...provide views never before seen...link itself to others.[24] We are not denying the movement of earlier endeavors. It is the finding of new and different commitments that enhances living. Even good health care includes responsibilities and tasks involving exercise for the patient.

The experiment of giving plants to two groups of patients in a nursing home is a case in point.[25] One group was told to just enjoy the beauty of the gifts; the second group was given small responsibilities, including care of the plants. Results? The well-being improved for those who had work to do, but within two years most patients who were pampered had died.

The departure of a Friday paycheck and the subsequent monthly arrival of a Social Security payment has meaning, but it is not of the ultimate variety. "There is no retirement from God's calling"[26] and we in the church can remind the elder that our baptism with its vocational call was for a lifetime.[27]

Suggested Reading:

Leisure a Spiritual Need, Leonard Doohan

No Retirement: Devotions on Christian Discipleship for Older People, Lillian Reynolds

Creative Communion: Toward a Spirituality of Work, Joe Holland

Grace: God's Work Ethic, Paul Johnson

Church Resource #11: Questions for Group Discussion

• Do you believe elders earn any entitlements?

• Can you name two jobs that you do which bring satisfaction?

• If you could change one thing about retiring, what would it be?

• Do you think that if women achieved total equality in the work market that they will then experience the male's shorter life span?

• What is an ideal age to retire?

• Do you relate to work associates the same as to church friends?

• What part do achievement and competition have in the life of the older adult?

• Does your employment feel like a calling or a job?

• Was your Grandfather's concept of work the same as yours?

• If aging were viewed as a career, would this raise our vision of getting older?

• Is there ever a right to be lazy?

• Does our culture reward all types of work equally?

• If due to technological innovation, there were a mass return to working at home, would any changes be felt in family, church, or community?

• Do you think the Protestant work ethic is still in effect?

12

READING LITERARY GEMS

When meaninglessness threatens at any age, the discouraged man or woman often turns to what another has considered important. In reading a novel or famous short story, it often comes as a surprise that what is shared on the printed page is helpful in a mysterious way. Time becomes three dimensional in the "communication of shared meaning"[1] as literature plays a key role in this compact viewing of ourselves and others.

Those of us embarked on new program ideas dealing with aging can find a source of inspiration and helpful perspective from the true or imaginary story skillfully told. Persons brought to life by a skilled writer can lead to awareness of real folk around us. We can rely on the author to say it for us. The reading itself can become a source of meaning to specific elders, or it can enhance a specific program purpose. So often, an indirect look at things forgotten, subtle, or too painful to face, takes on new meaning when told through a fictional character or event. The value of unchanging themes in a changing world gives permanence and hope.

Within a committee a varied scope of reading ability need not be a problem. For those who tend not to read (a habit reflecting early life patterns—educative and social) then quotes read or summarized, or chapters photocopied may be enough; for those members more informed and educated a more advanced form or method of participation might be applied.

Three notes of awareness here: according to Donald Deffner, educated adults, with their characteristics of integrative thinking, thirst for relevance, tolerance of diversity, impatience with waste, etc., are prone to prejudice against faith. What is needed is to "lift up true Christianity as broader, intellectually honest, and more humane and liberating," than their former experience of "closed, judgmental and anti-intellectual expression."[2] Good literature can help to do this.

Second, while literature is not always complimentary to people, it can be revealing of human nature. It can also be faulty or unfair. An author has the liberty to punish "for inappropriate behavior by describing negative physical aging characteristics."[3] Third, a delight in catchy phraseology—consider "generation gaps" and "quantum leaps"—can mask our need to mesh and mend age differences or to evaluate. Rhetoric can distort as well as authenticate. Words can also, through time, change in meaning. What is needed for everyone is a kind of reading that is reflective, not fact-collecting. Reading that speaks to all, and is outside of a rigid time frame can be substituted for formal kinds of learning. It plugs into the more psychological "knowing" which is the heart of effective education. There is a Tom Sawyer, a Mary Poppins, a Job, an Owen Meany in each of us. The methods of using poetry, drama, short story, letter, and biography, in our churches can vary. Any committee can use discretion, whether to use these readings as conversation starters, examples to hammer home a point, or as a built-in requirement for a study course. From a method for serious clinical work to light-hearted brainstormer, the other choices are many. Small groups for adults, for example, can take different forms. There could be: 1) Readers who meet monthly at homes or churches solely to discuss special books. A yearly list can be prepared, and members would have an opportunity to discuss and reflect on questions posed, which might include the implication of faith in the main character, or what motivated that person to act in a certain way.

This type may best be led by a person competent in guiding discussions, and able to provide thoughtful background about the author. 2) A small group with therapeutic intent, perhaps under the guidance of a trained professional, might discuss more emotionally based issues as portrayed in short excerpts. The more personalized issues of death, self-esteem, or finding God in particular circumstances, are appropriate. 3) Groups within a healthcare facility may first need encouragement to read. Often influenced by negative attitudes, their feelings about themselves (as worthless and inferior) may create barriers.[4] On the other hand, they "demonstrate unparalleled capacities for high level comprehension and interpretation."[5] The older adult with physical impairment can continue to be mentally alert and emotionally intact.

All of us can think of the literary gems as tools that open the soul to awareness. With this purpose in mind, the inclusion of poem, quote or story can be easily incorporated into sermon, Sunday School lesson, study program or workshop.

Here are a few. They are meant to trigger possibilities for those hard at work planning appropriate and useful. I invite not only investigation but enjoyment.

Prize Tomatoes by Anne Rosner. Walter, a retired businessman, living with his married daughter, finds her over-protectiveness damaging. Generally polite and accommodating, but with changed late-life viewpoints, his joyful gardening becomes the focus for successful rebellion. The good intentions are painfully familiar to those of us caught up in family caregiving.
Short story.

Walking Across Egypt by Clyde Edgerton. A spunky, endearing member of Listre Baptist interprets "to the least of these my brethren" to include a dogcatcher and a teen delinquent. Her habit of feeding all her acquaintances becomes a metaphor of God's love for the world. Mattie's ability to laugh at herself

masks the elder's common needs for independence, the centrality of organized religion, and the difficulty of maintaining private living space.
Fiction.

The Desert Blooms by Sarah-Patton Boyle. Believing herself adequately prepared for any eventuality, a single, educated woman moves to a different town only to discover her age and perspective is viewed as deficient. How she actively finds new meaning following despair is inspirational. Note: the church plays a major role in her pain and adjustment.
Non-fiction.

The Stone Angel by Margaret Lawrence. Hagar Shipley, a proud woman of 90, is strapped by her past and the memories of a reckless marriage until she experiences an "epiphany," a dramatic change, when her pastor—on a rare private request—renders an early musical version of Psalm 100. A classic.
Fiction.

Forever Fifty by Judith Viorst. Contemporary poet pokes fun at the common experiences of middle-aged women. Her "AT MY AGE" reflects assumptions. Realness of the trivialities wake us up to more important things.
Poetry.

Momento Mori by Muriel Spark. The same mysterious phone call is received by a mix of aged characters. Responses vary, and the reader is caught up in a clever, often humorous look at aging.
Fiction.

King Lear by William Shakespeare. A play about a common, identifiable family experience. On retirement, a king seeks to divide his kingdom between three daughters according to love.

Nothing proceeds as planned. Jealousy, disinheritance, and death are the unpredicted.
Tragedy.

The Summer of the Great Grandmother by Madeline L'Engle. In the context of a large family, a gifted author of adult non-fiction and juvenile stories shares memories and incidentals that reflect universal experience.
Non-fiction.

The Plum Tree by Mary Ellen Chase. It is not only the residents of the homes for the aged that have difficulties. A tribute to a nurse.
Classic novella.

Praisesong for the Widow by Paule Marshall. A series of strange events cause Avey Johnson, who is black, and a widow of means, to leave a luxurious cruise, and with the aid of an unlikely old man, pursue her spiritual heritage. Working through grief means new identity, risks, and a brand-new future.
Fiction.

The Marriage Feast by Par Lagerkvist. An aura of heavenly light blesses this late life marriage of "an insignificant little man" and a plain seamstress. A rare picture of intimacy.
Short story.

At Seventy, A Journal by May Sarton. A well-known contemporary author poet and lecturer shares her daily thoughts about the value of her creative work, the appreciation of our natural world, the importance of good friends and the seeing of her aging self as "more myself than I have ever been."
Non-fiction.

A Theory of Knowledge by Joyce Carol Oates At last. In retire-

ment there is time to write the book of his dreams. Although physically weak, Prof. Weber finds the abuse of a child changes the form of his final contribution.
Short story.

Survival of the Spirit by Ruth Howard Gray. At age 85 Ruth, capable of walking with a cane, enters a retirement home of her choice. The diary she kept highlights the indignities—feeling betrayed, being restricted, crying dry tears, etc. Still capable of thinking, feeling and evaluating, she moves elsewhere and attests to the value of knowing one's spiritual resources.
Non-fiction.

Tell Me a Riddle by Tillie Olsen. The emotional isolation of a dying woman reflects not just a physical condition but a lifelong history of fatigue from many demands. Conflicts with her husband as to preferred place for retirement reveal a history of poor communication.
Fiction.

The Oath by Elie Wiesel. The sole survivor of the village of Kolvillage is an old wanderer who chooses to give up his past to save a young stranger who is considering suicide. Forceful writing.
Fiction.

The creativity of all ages reflects the hand of God. The reading or sharing of others' words and feelings can inspire the expressive modes within all of us. The elder is no exception. Especially tuned into the seeing, feeling, experiencing of God's presence, the elder may, in his or her shrinking world, at last be able to respond with his or her own latent or unknown abilities. Participation is not limited to being the listener or the viewer or the passive bystander. With endless dishes or diapers no longer calling, there may be time at last to feel distinctly joined to

God's creative processes. Dare we say the urge or drive for self-expression lengthens the desire for living life to its fullest?

But, tired of the metaphors of winter, wizened, wasted, the late-blooming elder wants instead, on occasion, the truth that lies in portrayals of the person as winsome, wise and witty. Sometimes whittled down by loss and often choice, creative efforts bloom—but not for cash. These express the soul, the spirit, the satisfied self. We have seen it so many times, evidenced in written word, painted picture, simpler lifestyle, keen observation:

> the desire for simplicity is leading some of us to value once more skills nearly lost, and to search out natural expressions of creativity. When the rediscovery of these skills emerges not from a wistful or nostalgic longing for the past but from a yearning to express the divine within ourselves, then we learn to live more simply and to pray in a more integrated fashion. Our creativity will become our prayer.[6]

It is no longer a question of possibility but of choice as to creativity in our later years. Indeed, history has proved that old age can be a time for developing talents and abilities, not allowing skills to decline.[7] A college president concluded that there is a "surge in the sixties" that defies conventional belief.[8]

The artistic as well as the literary analogy can be an effective teacher. Take the imaging of the simple "wheel." Henri Nouwen uses this familiar form for characterizing aging, saying "no one of its spokes is more important than others, but together they make the circle full and reveal the hub as the core of its strength."[9] Douglas Steere, famed spiritual leader, uses the wheel to define corporate worship. With God as the hub, he says, "the nearer the spokes of the wheel are to the center, the nearer they are to each other."[10] The church is a place where we can share what others have said and done, and then get on with our own contributions.

Church Resource #12: A Time for Everything

For everything there is a season, and a time for every matter
under heaven:
a time to be born, and a time to die;
a time to plant, and a time to pluck up what is planted;
a time to kill, and a time to heal;
a time to break down, and a time to build up;
a time to weep, and a time to laugh;
a time to mourn, and a time to dance;
a time to throw away stones, and a time to gather stones together;
a time to embrace, and a time to refrain from embracing;
a time to seek, and a time to lose;
a time to keep, and a time to throw away;
a time to tear, and a time to sew;
a time to keep silence, and a time to speak;
a time to love, and a time to hate;
a time for war, and a time for peace.[11]

Use these poetic words to cultivate awareness of differences between cultural clock times and God's many messages of
right times.

13

CAREGIVING AS AN ACTIVE CHRISTIAN AFFAIR

The final rationale for the church's caring about those of all ages is rooted in the scriptures. The good samaritan parable (Luke 10:29–37) causes us to rethink who exactly is our neighbor; like the common sparrow each of us is valuable in God's view (Matthew 10:31). Likewise, created in God's image (Genesis 1:27) means we, in turn, are to care about others in the community. With a new way of relating promised (Galatians 3:26-29), there will be many blessings to those who hear and respond (Matthew. 5:1–11). Can we not apply these messages in both a personal and corporate way?

The church is the place or context created by God in which we are to do what is to be done.[1] Thomas Robb, Presbyterian, Executive Director of the National Interfaith Coalition on Aging, drawing from Paul Minear's *Images of the Church in the New Testament* reminds us of work God calls the church to do. It is seen in the early terms of *kerygma* (proclamation), *koinonia* (community sharing), and *diakonia* (service).[2] Moreover, from the beginning, the elders were part of the church—experiencing fellowship, sharing belongings, suffering, giving service.[3] By definition today, the elderly who need our help include not only the disabled and physically frail, but those who are socially, economically, and psychologically independent.[4]

According to Robb, our reasons for reaching out in the twentieth century to elders have been categorized into his light-hearted "Ain't it Awful" Argument, "Ain't it Wonderful" Argument, and "Because it's There" Argument. The first points to the common idea that old people are all sick, poor or lonely. The second suggests old age is wonderful, meaning the consumer market can profit from it and control it. The third points to the startling growth statistics showing thirty million Americans as age 65 or older. He suggests, instead, a return to an "Argument from Design," meaning, God's purpose.[5] But roadblocks remain.

The assumptions that (a) all persons automatically care or know how to do so, and (b) we all know what unloving care is can be deceiving. Few guidelines exist. Caregivers know little about the aging process.[6] And as to identifying unloving care, are we aware that according to a ranking public health official, it is more difficult to measure and control quality care in the nursing home, for example, than it is to provide it?[7] The culprit is public policy more than it is not caring!

So, what can it possibly mean to be a contemporary giver of care? We could turn to literature, as suggested earlier, and read stories like the powerful one of the single middle-aged professional who unintentionally became totally absorbed in Maudie's incredible survival.[8] One small outreach of caring led to total involvement in the life of another. The caregiver's perspective on life and love was changed forever. Or, we could recall the many possible kinds of caregivers that there can be.[9] These are described as: crisis caregiver, occasional caregiver, full-time, primary or casual caregiver. Then again, we could move from the why to a more philosophical stance, such as "what now is my path?"[10]

We are, at least, all familiar with the local figure rushing, hot pie in hand, to an obvious crisis situation. We are quick to respond to such catastrophes as fire and flood, but "social erosion and pollution of the human spirit should bring a new sense of quickening to each of us."[11] We must admit we often care more about the health and well-being of the family cat!

So, we need to draw a distinction between those occasional acts of concern and the growing into a broader understanding of what "caring about" another can mean. The difference between the Marys and Marthas of the world have plagued people for centuries. Giving and receiving need not be limited or interpreted as only monetary or material handouts. Neither does it need be singular. Group effort can have a wider scope of meaning.

We need to admit that the direction to take may be best defined by active elders themselves. Father Henri Nouwen, known for his insight into spiritual matters, says the elder can teach us. "They" say we mix up cure with care.[12] "They often return from a clinic cured but depersonalized."[13] Thus, we need to put emphasis on caring being a person-centered ministry. We could begin by seeing persons as encompassing four parts: an emotional self, a physical self, a social self, and a spiritual self.[14]

For the physical self, we can provide practical supportive services. Within the church, these may include telephone reassurance, tutoring, visitation, home repair, legal help, and nutrition. These are, perhaps, the easiest needs to identify. Outside the church, there are local agencies as well as national groups with local chapters that also offer practical help and need to be identified. These would include interfaith efforts in the town or state that may already have programs and budgets in operation. Involvement in these would mean learning to work together in caring projects.

The church's part may be in connecting the person with the appropriate existing group. Many elders living alone are unaware of available services. A few groups that reach out to others include: SCORE, RSVP, FOSTER GRANDPARENTS and HOSPICE. The Older American Act of 1965 with its many amendments brings funds for services to major areas of the country. Contact the nearest listing in the yellow pages.

Many adults within and outside the church are choosing

volunteerism, giving increasing amounts of time to others and finding satisfaction in doing so.[15] "How old is too old to be a volunteer?" asks the authors of *Success Over Sixty*.[16] They answer with the story of a dinner dance benefiting the United Hospital Fund where each lead volunteer was over ninety! (These included a 93 year old man still going to the office every day and a 92 year old woman who had just written 40 letters on behalf of the fund!)

Volunteerism can take many forms. Often it is not a random thing; it sometimes requires the church to design new roles or to train and develop new approaches. It can mean finding persons with strong organizational skills who will contribute time, energy, skill and love to ensure regular, reliable service. It also means recognizing that the institutionalized and homebound can also volunteer in special ways.[17]

To confuse our understanding, the concept of entitlement in caretaking has come on the scene.[18] The programs and public institutions in our history were never designed to reintegrate the elderly into our culture. They were intended to reinforce the idea of separating from the community.[19] Powerlessness has resulted; the elders now being "bureaucratically diseased and dependent." [20]

So, again, we must be on our guard against a limited vision of what care is about. It is necessary to move beyond services to focusing on what one theologian calls "new possibilities of elders becoming centers of freedom and love."[21] This suggests that perhaps there are tasks that only the church is able to do. "We're perpetuating the mindlessness when we provide only the bingo games." [22] We must look beyond practical services to emotional and spiritual needs.

Small groups for those with particular concerns, led by a professional, can give moral support, and provide a secure place for sharing troublesome issues of a personal nature. Likewise, counseling by seminary-trained leaders can be an important part of any caring ministry. To know that illness is often interpreted as failure within our culture calls for the listener to be sensitive to what the elder may indirectly imply.

Pastoral care and counseling can take different forms. One can be supportive in a crisis situation; another may provide more in the way of self-understanding.[23] Care is expressed by bringing faith and hope to the elder. Sometimes brought up to believe that one does not actively seek out support for emotional needs, the elder must often rely on the church leader initiating or spelling out the availability or openness to this kind of relationship.

Outside the church, and within the health-care system, the elder is dependent on variables. For example, knowledge that medical care can include inadequate attention because a patient is seen as old, poor, or with an uninteresting disease, is disturbing.[24] The physician's statement that "we are trained to be heroes"[25] does not jibe with an elder's need for treatment of a chronic condition versus an acute condition.[26] Chronic, of course, includes heart, cancer, stroke, diabetes, kidney failure, etc. Neither does the statement coincide with the church's task of humility and service.

Most important, and also often outside the immediate church awareness, is the family member as caregiver. (The word "family" will be used here to include not only the traditional nuclear concept but what has become a wider group of persons caring for each other.) Much is currently being written about this kind of caregiver because of the increased number of family members who are finding themselves in this position. Real problems often arise. Read that best-selling novel about young Isabel[27] who finds difficulty in adjusting to her own needs after spending eleven years caring for an aging Catholic father. Moreover, we must draw a distinction between our caregiving ministry to not only the elder within the family, but to the person doing the daily round of tending, the one feeling overwhelmed, completely responsible, and with little support.

While RESPITE[28] groups to help those involved in this kind of care are rapidly forming in many places, most caregivers find it difficult to define limits of what they can do. Raising the question of whether a Christian can love too much remains a concern. This is also a title of a book.[29]

Caregiving within the home raises sensitive issues which are especially stress-related to both elder and caregiver. When baby drools we approach, gladly, with helping hand; when Grandma drools, repulsed, we generally move away. Because mumps and measles have changed to carcinoma and cardiovascular disease, we become uncomfortable. We seem caught in learned cultural responses. Our many ethnic backgrounds influence what will be our method and attitude of care. Most of all, there will be new uncertainties, decisions to be made, changes in routines, role shifts, and a desperate need for good communication.[30] Does the sight and experience of illness and disability represent an unresolved difficulty in the church's understanding of loving and shared living? Have we become decadent in our preference for only shared laughter and youthful physical beauty? Are we unable to respond to need because our own infinitude is threatened? Is the absence of usefulness still haunting our efforts to offer loving care?

There are new concepts of caregiving being developed. Programs of service credits for service given sometimes alleviate the elders' economic state; the newly formed Eldercare Locator program will assist when friend or relative lives in another geographic area. See your local state Health and Human Services Department.

We in the church could symbolize a special kind of family, seeing ourselves as also needy, aging, and part of the mutuality of caring.[31] Acting out love for others is an invitation to others to join in doing the same. It will become a form of evangelism without the ranting and raving, offering instead the loving, emphatic, and personal. Age-specific groups will melt away into a deeper meaning of justice for all. The church's fourfold identity of chosenness, corporateness, caringness and celebrativeness will be apparent.[32] Our elders will have increased self-esteem because aging will seem a privilege.[33] When the old competitive ways of the different age groups dissolve into mutual caring, the recognition of the special gifts of each will be apparent.

The meaning of successful aging can be understood as sometimes simply "getting up each morning, being independent, . . .dressing, cooking, shopping, demanding and getting satisfaction from a hardhearted or indifferent doctor or welfare official."[34] Then the church will experience firsthand the kind of miracles that happen when people obey and trust God who for our sake experienced similar aloneness, suffering, and betrayal before divine purposes were miraculously revealed.

"We love because he first loved us," *I John 4:19.*

Suggested Reading:

Bible Readings for Caregivers, Betty Syverson

Family Caregivers & Dependent Elderly, Dianne Springer

Older Volunteers, Lucy Fischer and Kay Schaffer

Family Therapy with the Elderly, Elizabeth Neidhardt and Rose Allen

Church Resource #13: Addresses of Helpful Organizations

Alzheimer's Disease and Related Disorders Association
919 North Michigan Ave.
Chicago, IL 60611
(312) 335–8700

American Association of Retired Persons AARP
601 E. St. NW
Washington, D.C. 20049
(202) 434–2277

American Society of Aging ASA
833 Market St.
San Francisco, CA. 94103
(415) 882–2910

Elderhostel
75 Federal St.
Boston, MA 02110
(617) 426–7788

Gray Panthers
1424 16th St. NW
Washington, D.C. 20036
(202) 387–3111

Health and Human Services Department
Administration on Aging AoA
330 Independence Ave. SW
Washington, D.C. 20201

National Council on the Aging NCOA
and
National Interfaith Coalition NICA
409 Third St. SW
Washington, D.C. 20024
(202) 479–6665

National Hispanic Council on Aging
2713 Ontario NW
Washington, D.C. 20009
(202) 265–1288

National Hospice Organization NHO
1901 N. Moore St.
Arlington, VA 22209
(703) 243–5900

Older Women's League OWL
730 11th St. NW., Suite 300
Washington, DC 20001
(202) 783–6686

Retired Senior Volunteer Program RSVP
1100 Vermont Ave. NW
Washington, DC 20525
(202) 606–4851

National Caucus and Center on the Black Aged
1424 K. St. NW
Washington, DC 20005
(202) 637–8400

14

ADVOCACY

The concerned parishioner who wishes to take action within the public arena can find ways to do so.

I. Write a letter to: a newspaper or magazine
                      a company or organization
                      a consumer protection agency.

To find out the best way to do this effectively, write to AARP for their booklet entitled *How to Write a Wrong*. Another resource is a chapter in *Older Adult Ministry,* which includes an excellent chart on criteria for judging media representations and, a copy of strategies for eliminating ageism in the media. Try drafting your own sample plea or complaint. Then show it to a friend. From issues of abuse to consumer information, a letter placed in the correct hands can mean immediate action.

II. Get appointed to a board of commission.

III. Lobby for or against a bill.

The above means finding and gathering facts. It can also mean monitoring the status of a bill, and the mobilizing of others. Opportunities for direct contact with representatives is highly recommended.

IV. Check on the local nursing home.

When we visit cousin Nellie at Golden Acres, we may see or feel things that don't seem "right." There may not be dust balls under the bed or the smell of urine in the halls, but is there subtle evidence of mistreatment or insensitivity? Unfamiliar with, or intimidated by, institutional care, we may hesitate to speak out. This is not easy to do, though the desire to do so may be intense. The Ombudsman in your area is the one to contact.

One of the church's responsibilities is to alert the older adult to their rights. Justice has always been a prime theme of the scriptures. In this light we could define the function of the advocate as threefold: the correction of injustice, the positive pursuit of justice, and the prevention of injustice.[1] "We are called. . .to act as a thorn in the side of society, questioning, analyzing, evaluating, and then proposing and implementing change for the better, in the name of a higher vision for our world."[2]

Oh God, give us strength to refrain "from the unkind silence that is born of hardness of heart."[3]

15

CELEBRATING AGE AS REBIRTH OF WONDER

The church's business is loving. Though the world in which we live is rapidly changing, the good news of the creation, the incarnation and the resurrection remains the same. Though age-spans lengthen, we in the church continue to celebrate the lives of all our members. Tuned in to self-discovery, continued growth, and renewed responsibility as new images of late life, we anticipate a time of new learning for ourselves and for the others within our churches.

The role of education in our church today is heightened by the rapidly changing cultural influences. By moving away from often dated concepts of Christian education, the church can reclaim its role as an effective educator by recognizing the ability and the desire of the adult to learn and grow. After all, adults of all ages share the same ultimate concerns. In addition, the elder is available to us as teacher. Often coming from the highly organized business world, as well as having been refined through pain and the experience of life events, the elder represents a new kind of knowing, a non-worldly kind of wisdom. Those of us in the church will learn from them that we can no longer exist as mediocre, impersonal and self-centered people. We can learn that the only abiding satisfaction is a right relationship to God. But beginning any specialized ministries in our churches means facing cultural attitudes and sinful ways. Preliminaries that elicit change include identifying our own false assumptions, finding leadership for our well-thought-out programs, identifying levels of need, and locating the limited existing written resources. We desperately need the elders to keep us on course, to function as our compasses. To admit that elders constitute a majority in our churches, and that being marginalized is the fate of some of our members, suggests we take a closer look at a deepened interiority and what it could mean for us in our personal and corporate time together. A reexamination of foundational beliefs may be in order. If to know God counterbalances increased physical limitations; if the quality of life changes, then this must be communicated. The elders' gifts and contributions must be achnowledged and affirmed. Those who are in a state of increased awareness and are feeling a perpetual state of gratitude for all that has been, all that is, and all that will be, *can* make a difference in our churches. Life experienced as a time of increased sensitivity to God's world—as a time of greater commitment to causes of justice and peace—needs to be shared. This must be allowed to flow into our hearts, our missions, our minds, so that it becomes intelligible in our often violent, competitive, youth-oriented world. Though we learn from tradition and doctrine, direct experience in our churches also teaches.

As we grow in our understanding of the aging process, many words must be updated. In addition to the word "wisdom," perhaps we need to find a new way to look at Christian maturity. The ability to reflect, and the critical analysis of self is a positive trait that eventually enriches others. We are all called to constant reevaluation, not to complacency. The oft-used metaphor of life as a journey continues through the late life developmental stages. We remember this when we look in the mirror and are tempted to pluck our first sign of greying finitude rather than think of its meaning. But life is not only a spiritual journey. It is also, always, a movement forward.[1] Much of God's work awaits completion by us.

Practical matters such as housing, decent food and access to friendly services continue to be prime issues in our churches. To be acquainted with the living condition options for all God's people, and to acknowledge the problems of changing family structures as well as the value of relationships with all ages is our continuing human agenda.

The issues concerning elder women are overwhelming. Many are poor, widowed, or belong to minority groups. These persons will need our immediate and special attention. Even feminist theologians have been slow to address particular issues here, though "double jeopardy" is a term increasingly applied. Retirement, once a male gender affair, is now a major concern for countless women. New identification and new meaning can be given to issues of work and leisure when the church describes vocation as a life-long relationship to God.

Literature, with its emphasis on universal themes, can continue to provide helpful perspectives to church groups needing added inspiration for personal growth and program development. The creative efforts of young and old alike enrich our understanding and constantly point to God's continuing presence among us.

The currently popular stance of caregiving needs to be enlarged to a vision of deeper concern. Forms vary, but only the church with its deepened awareness of the servant model will find appropriate opportunities for unique methods of intervention. This can include individual advocacy involvement for those who prefer to lobby or monitor specific injustice. With the increases in the cost of living index, and the residing together of third and fourth generations, the demands and kinds of caregiving will skyrocket. Women, in particular, need to be prepared. Be on the alert.

Cultural problems will remain. That we are often more shaped by our culture and society than from our religious beliefs comes as a shock. We forget that what God wants and what our culture wants are in tension.

The future of the church will depend on individuals who are spiritually mature. They are the ones who recognize God as active in their lives, and they make the effort to interpret through the scriptures, the tradition, reason and experience what God's will is, at the same time acknowledging their sins of omission. They will be the illogical ones according to the standards of the culture, but the chosen ones according to God. They know who they are, and to whom they belong.

What is most conclusive from the study is the place of individual responsibility. The living and dying process of each and every one of us invites a new kind of relationship with God, and a continuing effort as to how to respond to both God and God's changing world regardless of age. The elder, in particular, may apply the familiar "to whom much is given, much is required." To the elder emerges the major task: to find out how to faithfully "be" young-old, old-old, or the frail elder, so that new models will enrich the next generations. It is also a time for evangelizing as we consider both the thirst of the many aged and the frenzy of the many young who do not seem to have strong religious values with which to face increased longevity.

While it is time to praise the many who pioneered the field within all our denominations, it is also time for increased attention by the theologian. Gerontological observations are not enough. Scientific concepts of total decline after ripeness are unfair. Instead, accepting the universality of both gain and loss seems to be one of the biblical messages.

Scholars warn us to note in the Old Testament stories about both the blessings and the diminishments of favorite figures. The long lives recorded still trigger curiosity. Stories about old age as a gift of God, and shortened life as a punishment from God are woven into our interpretations. We are assured that we are created in God's image, and that creation was good. Other scripture messages declare God's continual encounters with those of various chronological ages. Each person seemed valued, and from this we take heart. But, our stress on individualism has, among other things, moved the now long-living American to false impressions that life apart from the community of faith is adequate and purposeful. One task of the church may be to bring members, young and old, to a new awareness of interrelatedness as divine intent.

With the recognition of the limitations of this study comes the realization that much more needs to be acknowledged and evaluated. The reeducation of clergy, the need for more elder participation, the confronting of cultural definitions of the aged as useless and unimportant, are but a few general topics to be addressed. Implications for new kinds of ministry arise, such as assertiveness training for elders and rituals for the transitions of aging. Possibilities for meaningful programs include the socialization of elder singles who are seeking, not a dating service, but the shared exploration of life's deeper sorrows and joys. In addition, with the questioning of moral capabilities by some, and with the current emphasis on issues in medical ethics, as well as the growing resistance to public expenditure for elder needs, responses from those committed to the ways of Christ are in demand. It is my hope that a solid glossary will some day be compiled to aid in the religious teaching of relevant social and psychological issues.

Cousin Nellie may not want that microwave but she might strongly desire a ride to church on Sunday, or a definite way to participate in the joy of generativity. It is imperative that we get started. We must get to know her better if we are to recognize her needs, her pain, her talents, and her wisdom garnered from a lengthy partnership with God. The church of the third century, according to the famed letter of Diognetus, was known by its loving actions based on its awareness of belonging to God. It seems that Christians, who were a persecuted minority, couldn't be distinguished by custom or language, but were simply good neighbors. They were not seen as subversive, but as people who frankly admitted their citizenship was not of this world. Churches do have choices. Today, as then, the church demands inclusion, interdependence, and contributions of all ages on the deepest levels. Today, we, too, with God's guidance, can find ways to live out God's word of love in the world.

The meaning of aging is complex. The miracle of growth, life, and death are mysteries that belong only to God. But we do remember the words, "unless we become as little children." That image suggests not physical resemblance by age, but adoption of an attitude of openness and receptivity to God's calling. It requires that special kind of knowing that comes from accumulated experience when "being" is valued over "doing."

The awareness that death is approaching generally changes the meaning of who we are. A growing awareness of finitude reveals a trust in God's purposes for all. It means following the divine example of the cross, learning hard lessons of selflessness and caring, as well as the acceptance of grace.

While the Christian perspective means compassionate acknowledgement of losses, the church can also view changes as challenges, finding strength and sustenance from the cohesiveness of believers, from the indwelling of the Spirit, and from hope in the promises made. The fundamental task of the church, communal in nature, is to find new metaphors for aging.[2] These must have contemporary meaning for both churches and elders. In our present darkness someone has suggested the comparison of the elder to a beacon, beckoning us in spite of our tendencies toward disobedience. We, in turn, can be reminders to the elder who tends to forget God's personal involvement; we will function as the embodiment of Christ to that marginalized 95 percent experiencing limitations, social isolation, despair or discouragement.

We *can* lift up the millions aging in our churches. We *can* move from a self-centered remembrance to both increased awareness and thanksgiving for the many who are aging with difficulty and those who are positive life-affirming witnesses to God's coming kingdom.

We *can* learn to move away from "doing for" to a stance of

"with" and "beside," truly acknowledging the other in the pew, the neighborhood, the global community. That a treasured conversation with an elder took place just yesterday is a positive sign.

Many questions have been raised. In this study, we have seen that our times reflect unfamiliar conditions that are not easily addressed by our churches. When Ettie Mae Green[3] recently attributed her 114 years to a daily milkshake and "good, clean living" we might wonder what exactly did she mean? Questions breed questions. We need to know *how* to go from Blythe's words about cultural self-concept as only nuisance[4] to Barbara Myerhoff's primary conclusive traits of vitality and flexibility. According to the anthropologist's stimulating personalized account[5] of a Jewish urban ghetto of elders in southern California, the primacy of religious ritual and practice deeply effected how diminished lives can be lived out.

Who *is* old? Does it matter? The view of any congregation come Sunday morning is evidence of God with us. All ages confess and praise but it is the elders who are "purged of the clutter of egocentric striving, open to the whisper of God calling us into being."[6]

Thanks Be To God!

Suggested Reading:

The Church's Ministry with Older Adults, Blaine Taylor

A Gathering of Hope, Helen Hayes

Nice Things about Growing Older, William Meyer

Telling Your Story, Exploring Your Faith, B.J. Hateley

NOTES

1. Getting Caught in Cultural Norms

[1] Martin E. Marty, *Cultural Antecedents to Contemporary American Attitudes toward Aging,* in **Ministry with the Aging,** William Clements, ed. (Cambridge: Harper & Row, 1981), 57.

[2] Carole Haber, **Beyond Sixty-Five: The Dilemma of Old Age in America's Past** (Cambridge: Cambridge University Press, 1983), 49.

[3] John Demos, *Old Age in Early New England,* in **Aging, Death, and the Completion of Being,** David D. Van Tassel, ed. ([n.p.]: University of Pennsylvania Press, 1979), 131.

[4] Cotton Mather, cited in Demos, 119.

[5] Demos, 129.

[6] David H. Fischer, **Growing Old in America,** The Bland-Lee Lectures delivered at Clark University (New York: Oxford University Press, 1977).

[7] Robert Butler, **Why Survive?** (New York: Harper & Row, 1975), 7–10.

[8] Frank Nuessel, Jr., The Language of Ageism, **Gerontologist** 22 (June '82): 274.

[9] Dychtwald, Kenneth, **Age Wave** (Los Angeles: Jeremy Tarcher, 1989), 8.

[10] Linda Vogel, **The Religious Education of Older Adults** (Birmingham, AL: Religious Education Press, 1984), 179.

2. Confirming the Strength of Diversity

[1] Charles Bruning, *The Hypotheses Paper*, **Faith Development in**

the Adult Life Cycle, Kenneth Stokes, ed. (New York: W.H. Sadlier, 1982), 28.

[2] Linda George and Elizabeth Clipp, *Subjective Components of Aging Well, Generations* XV 1 (Winter 1991): 59.

[3] Kathleen Fischer, *Winter Grace* (New York: Paulist Press, 1985), 16.

3. Targeting the Middle-Aged Parishioner

[1] J.R.P. Sclater, *The Interpreters' Bible* IV *The Book of Psalms,* Exposition, 127.

[2] David Maitland, *Looking Both Ways: A Theology of Midlife* (Atlanta: John Knox Press, 1983), 21.

[3] Les Steele, *On The Way: A Practical Theology of Christian Formation* (Grand Rapids: Baker Book House, 1990), 166.

[4] James Fowler, *Becoming Adult, Becoming Christian* (San Francisco: Harper & Row, 1984), 28.

[5] *Peddling Youth Over the Counter, Newsweek* 115 (March 5, 1990): 50–52.

[6] Robert Peck, *Psychological Development in the Second Half of Life,* in *Middle Age and Aging,* Bernice Neugarten, ed. (Chicago: University of Chicago Press, 1968), 231.

[7] Eugene Bianchi, *Aging As a Spiritual Journey* (New York: Crossroad, 1990), 231.

[8] Kenneth Stokes, ed., *Faith Development in the Adult Life Cycle* (New York: W.H. Sadlier, 1982), 10.

[9] J. Conrad Glass and Elizabeth Knott, *An Analysis of the Effectiveness of Workshop on Aging in Changing Middle Aged Adults' Attitudes toward the Aged* (NRTA/AARP, Andros Foundation, 1981). This study was done in North Carolina at workshops in 10 locations. The sample consisted of 162 adults. Central purpose was to see if planned educational experiences could change attitudes toward older persons.

[10] Les Steele, 170.

[11] David Maitland, *Looking Both Ways,* 3.

[12] For example, see *It Had To Be Done So I Did It,* a project funded by The New Hampshire Humanities Council.

[13] A fine hymn resource is Kenneth Osbeck's *101 Hymn Stories,* (Grand Rapids, MI.: Kregel Publications, 1982).

[14] An ecumenical ministry, *New Beginnings Singles Group,* has been successfully developed at the United Church of Christ in Norwell, MA. Leadership is both paid and volunteer.

[15] Based on one of the many versions of a tale for children.

4. Church Programming as Educational Process

[1] Linda Jane Vogel, *Religious Education of Older Adults* (Birmingham, AL: Religious Education Press, 1984), 57–62.

[2] Lewis Aiken, *Later Life,* 2nd ed. (New York: Holt, Rinehart & Winston, 1982) 81.

[3] Leon McKenzie, *Religious Education of Adults* (Birmingham, AL: Religious Education Press, 1982), 32.

[4] Defined by Malcolm Knowles, in Linda Jane Vogel, 55.

[5] Leo Missinne, in *Aging and Spirituality*, American Society of Aging. II 3 (October 1990): 3.

[6] Eugene Bianchi, *Aging As a Spiritual Journey* (New York: Crossroad, 1990), 225–242.

[7] Robert Butler, *Why Survive?* (New York: Harper & Row, 1975), 88.

[8] Tilman Smith, *In Favor of Growing Older* (Scottsdale, PA: Herald Press, 1981), 81.

[9] Rochel Berman and Ellen Geis, *Intergenerational Contact: Theological and Social Insights*, *Religious Education* 70 6 (November–December 1975): 661–75.

[10] Tim Spafford, *As Our Years Increase: Loving, Caring, Preparing for Life Past 65* (New York: Harper/Collins, 1991).

[11] Evelyn E. Whitehead and James D. Whitehead, *Christian Life Patterns* (New York: Doubleday, 1979), 221.

[12] Described in *Wholistic Theology As a Conceptual Foundation for Services for the Oldest Old,* in *Spiritual Maturity in Later Years,* James Seeber, ed. (New York: Haworth Press, 1990), 245.

[13] Donald Miller, *Adult Religious Education and the Aging,* in *Ministry with the Aging* William Clements, ed. (New York: Haworth Press, 1989), 245.

[14] Blaine Taylor, *The Church's Ministry with Older Adults* (Nashville: Abingdon Press, 1984), 90.

5. Getting Started

[1] Eugene Bianchi, *Aging As A Spiritual Journey* (New York: Crossroad, 1990), 13.

[2] Arthur Becker, *Ministry with Older Persons* (Minneapolis: Augsburg House, 1986), 20.

[3] One example is Erdman Palmore's, *Facts on Aging: A Short Quiz, Gerontologist* 17 (August 1977): 315–20.

[4] William Cohen, *The Art of the Leader* (Englewood Cliffs, NJ: Prentice Hall, 1990).

[5] J. Edward Carothers, *The Paralysis of Mainstream Protestant Leadership* (Nashville: Abingdon Press, 1990).

[6] David Oliver, *Preparing Clergy and Professional Religious Educators to Work with Older Adults,* in *Implications of Age,* Papers from a symposium, April 27–29, 1988. Pittsburgh Theological Seminary, 25.

[7] Alfred S. Fox, *Tapping the Resources of Time, Christianity Today* 25 1–12, (Jan.–June, 1981): 617.

[8] Donald Greggs and Judy Walther, *Christian Education in the Small Church* (Valley Forge: Judson Press, 1988) Ch. 5.

[9] James McDaniel, *Planning and Developing Older Adult Programs,* in *Older Adult Ministry: A Resource for Program Development* (Atlanta: Presbyterian Publishing House, 1987), 57.

[10] Ibid. 47.

[11] Pat Moore, *Disguised* (Waco, TX: Word Books, 1985).

[12] Blaine Taylor, *The Church's Ministry with Older Adults* (Nashville: Abingdon Press, 1985), 42.

[13] Linda Jane Vogel, *The Religious Education of Older Adults* (Birmingham, AL: Religious Education Press, 1984), 147–149.

[14] Sheldon Tobin, ed., *Enabling the Elderly* (Albany: State University of New York Press, 1986), 46.

6. Empowering Discipleship

[1] Frank Hutchison, *Aging Comes of Age* (Louisville: Westminster/John Knox Press, 1991), 85.

[2] Anne Foner, *Aging and Old Age: New Perspectives* (Englewood Cliffs, N.J.: Prentice-Hall, 1986), 134.

[3] William Clements, *Care and Counseling of the Aging* (Philadelphia: Fortress Press, 1979); Appendix A. *Self-Image and Public Image of Older Persons,* 67.

[4] Shared by Roderick MacDonald in *Content Analysis of Perceptions of Aging as Reproduced by the News Media,* presented at the 26th annual meeting of The Gerontology Society.

[5] Lou Cottin, *Elders in Rebellion: A Guide to Senior Activism* (Garden City, NY: Anchor Press/Doubleday, 1979), 79.

[6] Margaret Hall, *Religion and Aging, Journal of Religion and Health,* 24 1 (Spring 1985): 74.

[7] Kathleen Fischer, *Winter Grace* (New York: Paulist Press, 1985), 11.

[8] David Maitland, *Looking Both Ways: A Theology for Mid-Life* (Atlanta: John Knox Press, 1985), 153–158.

[9] James Anderson, *Taking Heart: Empowering Older Adults for Community Ministries: A Handbook* (Washington, D.C.: Cathedral College of the Laity, 1987), 9.

[10] James J. Seeber, *Beginnings of a Theology for Aging, Generations* XIV 4 (Fall 1990): 48–50.

[11] Kenneth Hougland, *Liberation from Age-ism: The Ministry of Elders, Christian Century* 91 (March 27, 1974): 340–2.

7. Looking at the Religious Life of Older Adults

[1] David Maitland, *Aging: Time for New Learning* (Atlanta: John Knox Press, 1987), 117.

[2] Barbara Payne, *Religion and the Elderly in Today's World*, in *Ministry with the Aging,* William Clements, ed. (Cambridge: Harper & Row, 1981), 154.

[3] Payne, 157.

[4] Payne, 165.

[5] A study, *The Household of Faith,* by Ann Taves concerning Roman Catholic devotions in mid-nineteenth century America includes a long list of prayerbooks published in the U.S. between 1770–1880.

[6] See, for example, *In the Footsteps of the Mystics,* Henry Simmons. (New York: Paulist Press, 1992).

[7] Jean Laporte, "The Elderly in the Life and Thought of the Early Church," in *Ministry with the Aging* William Clements, ed.

(Cambridge: Harper & Row, 1981), 52.

[8] Excerpted in *Revelations: Diaries of Women,* Mary Jane Moffat and Charlotte Painter, eds. (New York: Vintage Books, 1975), 363.

[9] Janet Belsky, *The Psychology of Aging* (Monterey, CA: Brooks/Cole Publishing Co., 1984).

[10] Isabel Docampo of the Baptist Senior Adult Ministries of Washington, D.C.

[11] In "Adapting Worship to Changing Needs," **Generations XIV 4** (Fall, 1990), 65–66.

[12] Evelyn Whitehead, "Religious Images of Aging," in *Aging and the Human Spirit: A Reader in Religion and Gerontology,* Carol LeFevre and Perry LeFevre, eds. (Chicago: Exploration Press, 1985), 65.

8. Rethinking Wisdom and Maturity

[1] Donald Wimmer, *Aging and Wisdom: East and West,* in *Teaching about Aging,* James Boskey, et al. ([n.p.] : University Press of America, 1982), 80.

[2] Christie Kiefer, *The Mantle of Maturity* (Albany: State University of New York Press, 1988), 8.

[3] David Maitland, *Aging: A Time for New Learning* (Atlanta: John Knox Press, 1987), vii.

[4] Boskey, 81.

[5] Roland Murphy, *Wisdom Literature and the Psalms* (Nashville: Abingdon Press, 1983), 34.

[6] Murphy, 32.

[7] Robert Davidson, *Wisdom and Worship* (Philadelphia: Trinity Press International, 1990), 11.

[8] Rachel Dulin, *A Crown of Glory: A Biblical View of Aging* (New York: Paulist Press, 1988), 73.

[9] Maitland, 132.

[10] C. Ellis Nelson, *How Faith Matures* (Louisville, KY: Westminster/John Knox Press, 1989), 61.

[11] Matthew Linn, Sheila Fabricant, Dennis Linn, *Healing the Eight Stages of Life* (New York: Paulist Press, 1987), 214.

[12] An interpretation of Augustine according to Nancy Jecker, *Adult Moral Development,* in **Generations** XIV 4 (Fall 1990): 21.

[13] The words of Erik Erikson as quoted in *Age Wave,* Kenneth Dychtwald (Los Angeles: Jeremy Tarcher, 1989), 345.

[14] In his *Memories, Dreams, Reflections,* he states: *"When people say I am wise or a sage, I cannot accept it,"* 355.

[15] Roberta Bondi, *To Love As God Loves* (Philadelphia: Fortress Press, 1987), 22, 23.

[16] *Addresses from the National Convocation on Older Adult Ministries,* The United Methodist Church, Fort Worth, TX, January 12–13, 1991.

[17] Ruth H. Jacobs, *Surviving and Thriving* (Milwaukee: Family Service of America, 1987).

[18] Found in *What's Inside You It Shines Out of You*, Marc Kaminsky (New York: Horizon Press, 1974), 219.

[19] Eveyln Underhill, *The Spiritual Life* (New York: Harper & Bros. 1958), 21.

[20] Found in Daniel Jenkins, *Christian Maturity and Christian Success* (Philadelphia: Fortress Press, 1982), chapter 12.

[21] Barbara Payne, *Spiritual Maturity and Meaning-Filled Relationships: A Sociological Perspective,* in *Spiritual Maturity in the Later Years,* James Seeber, ed. (New York: Haworth Press, 1990), 37.

[22] Erik Erikson, *Reflections on Dr. Borg's Life Cycle,* in *Aging, Death and the Completion of Being,* David Van Tassel, ed. (Philadelphia: University of Pennsylvania Press, 1979), 53.

[23] Evelyn Whitehead and James Whitehead, *Seasons of Strength,* Image Books (Garden City, NY: Doubleday and Co. Inc., 1984), chapter 5.

[24] Kathleen Fischer, *Winter Grace: Spirituality for the Later Years* (New York: Paulist Press, 1985), 32.

[25] Susanne Johnson, *Christian Spiritual Formation in the Church and Classroom* (Nashville: Abingdon Press, 1989), 110.

9. Spotlighting Place and Relationship

[1] David Moherg, *Religiosity in Old Age*, in *Middle Age and Aging, A Reader in Social Psychology,* Bernice Neugarten, ed. (Chicago: University of Chicago Press, 1968), 497.

[2] Ken Dychtwald, *Age Wave* (Los Angeles: Jeremy Tarcher, 1989), 134–136.

[3] Ibid. 156.

[4] Jo Horne, with Leo Baldwin, *Home-Sharing and Other Lifestyle Options,* AARP. (Glenview, IL: Scott, Foresman & Co., 1988), 143–151.

[5] Ibid., chapters 1–6. This described in detail, including advantages and disadvantages.

[6] Lou Cottin, *Elders in Rebellion* (Garden City, NY: Anchor Press/Doubleday, 1979), 79.

[7] Dychtwald, 139.

[8] Elena Newman, *Golden Years without a Care,* in *Insight on the News,* 8 2 (January 13, 1992): 14.

[9] Lois Wyse, *Funny, You Don't Look Like a Grandmother* (Thorndike, ME: Thorndike Press, 1989), 85.

[10] One example: *What Kind of Family Do You Have?* by Gretchen Super (Frederick, MD: Twenty-First Century Books, 1991), 14.

[11] Mary Jo Gibson, *Older Women Around the World* (Washington, D.C.: International Federation on Aging, 1985), 14.

[12] One example: Paul Tournier, *Learn to Grow Old* (Louisville, KY: Westminster/John Knox Press, 1990).

[13] Rebecca Adams, *A Look at Friendship and Aging,* in *Generations,* X 4 Summer 1986, 40–43.

[14] Bonnie Genevay, *Intimacy As We Age,* in *Generations,* X 4 (Summer 1986): 13.

[15] James Birren and K. Warner Schaie, eds., *The Psychology of Aging* (New York: Van Nostrand Reinhold Co., 1977), 376–377.

[16] M.F.K. Fisher, *Sister Age* (New York: Random House, 1984), 240.

[17] John Westerhoff, *Liturgy and Learning Through the Life Cycle* (New York: Seabury Press, 1980), chapter 10.

[18] See Sellner Edward's *Mentoring: A Ministry of Spiritual Kinship* (Notre Dame, IN: Ave Maria Press, 1990).

[19] Carole Haber, *Beyond 65* (Cambridge: Cambridge University Press, 1983), chapter 3 and 5.

[20] Mickey T. Friedman, *Housing Alternatives and Living Arrangements,* in *Ourselves Growing Older,* by Paul Brown Doress

and Diana Laskin Siegal. The Midlife and Older Women Book Project. (New York: Simon and Schuster, 1987), 154, 155.

10. Focusing on the Older Woman

[1] Kathleen Fischer, *Winter Grace: Spirituality for the Later Years* (New York/Mahwah: Paulist Press, 1985), 85.

[2] Kenneth Dychtwald, *Age Wave* (Los Angeles: Jeremy Tarcher, 1989), 222.

[3] Ibid. 224.

[4] Trends in formula writing, by Kathryn Weibel, in *Mirror, Mirror: Images of Women Reflected in Popular Culture* (Garden City, NY: Anchor Press/Doubleday, 1977), Anchor Books, chapter 1.

[5] Susan Tamke, *Human Values and Aging: The Perspective of the Victorian Nursery,* in *Aging and the Elderly: Humanistic Perspectives in Gerontology* Stuart Spicker, ed. (Atlantic Highlands, NJ: Humanities Press, 1978).

[6] Barbara Walker, *The Crone Woman of Age, Wisdom and Power* (San Francisco, Harper & Row, 1985).

[7] Dychtwald, 224.

[8] Jean Laporte, *The Elderly in the Life and Thought of the Early Church*, in *Ministry with the Aging*, William Clements, ed. (Cambridge: Harper & Row, 1981), chapter 3.

[9] Janet Belsky, *The Psychology of Aging* (Monterey, CA: Brooks/Cole Publishing Co., 1984), 203–206.

[10] Jerry Gerber, Janet Wolff, Walter Klores and Gene Brown. *Lifetrends: The Future of Baby Boomers and Other Aging Americans* (NY: Macmillan Publishing Co., 1989), 25.

[11] Arthur Kornhaber and Kenneth Woodward. *Grandparents/ Grandchildren: The Vital Connection* (Garden City, NY: Doubleday/ Anchor, 1981), 167–179.

[12] David Gutmann, *Reclaimed Powers: Toward a New Psychology of Men and Women in Later Life* (N.Y.: Basic Books, 1987).

[13] U.S. Bureau of the Census, Current Population Reports, Series P-60, No. 175. *Poverty in the United States: 1990* U.S. Government Printing Office, 1991.

[14] Carol Austin, *Aging Well: What Are the Odds?*, in **Generations,** XV 1 (Winter 1991): 73.

[15] Margaret Moody, ed., **Older Women Alone,** A Summary of the Conference sponsored by The Institute for the Study of Women in Transition, September 22–25, 1975 (Portsmouth, N.H.: The Institute Press, [n.d.]), 14.

[16] AARP **Bulletin,** 32, 10 (November, 1991): 1.

[17] Lillian Troll, *The Psycho-Social Problems of Older Women*, in **The World of the Older Woman,** "Conflict and Resolutions," Gari Lesnoff-Caravaglia, ed. (NY: Human Sciences Press, 1984), 24.

[18] Letita T. Alston and Jon Alston, *Religion and the Older Woman,* in **Aging and the Human Spirit: A Reader in Religion and Gerontology,** 2nd ed., Carol LeFevre and Perry LeFevre, eds. (Chicago: Exploration Press, 1985), 169.

[19] Fischer, 91.

[20] Kornhaber, 220.

[21] The New Oxford Annotated Bible, Isaiah 11:6.

11. Appraising the Value of Work and Leisure

[1] Max Weber, **The Protestant Ethic and Spirit of Capitalism** (New York: Charles Scribner's Sons, 1958).

[2] Kenneth Dychtwald, **Age Wave** (Los Angeles: Jeremy Tarcher, 1989), 121.

[3] Mary Wilkins Freeman's short story, in **Themes of Adulthood Through Literature,** Sharon Merriam, ed. (NY: Teachers College Press, Columbia University, 1983), 279–291.

[4] Witold Rybczynski, **Waiting for the Week-End** (NY: Viking, 1991).

[5] James Murphy, **Concepts of Leisure** (Englewood Cliffs: Prentice Hall, 1974), 61.

[6] Gabriel Moran, *Work, Leisure, and Religious Education*, in **Religious Education,** 74, 2. (Mar/Apr 1979): 167.

[7] Seward Hiltner, **Toward a Theology of Aging** (New York: Human Sciences Press, 1979). A special issue of **Pastoral Psychology,** 24, (Winter 1975): 229.

[8] Moran, 160.

[9] Josef Pieper, *Leisure: The Basis of Culture* (New York: Pantheon Books, 1952), 40.

[10] Aristotle, *Nicomachean Ethics,* Book X, (New York: Macmillan Publishing Co., 1962).

[11] Pieper, 56.

[12] Leonard Doohan, *Leisure a Spiritual Need* (Notre Dame, IN: Ave Maria Press, 1990), 99.

[13] John Zehring, *Making Your Life Count* (Valley Forge: Judson Press, 1980), 13.

[14] Bernice Neugarten and Dale Neugarten, *The Changed Meanings of Age,* in *Psychology Today,* 21 (May 1987): 29.

[15] Dychtwald, 121.

[16] Perry LeFevre, *Toward a Theology of Aging,* in *Aging and the Human Spirit: A Reader in Religion and Gerontology,* 2d edition. Carol Levre, Perry LeFevre, ed. (Chicago: Exploration Press, 1985), 48.

[17] Howard Walker, *Is Leisure the Church's Business?,* in *Spectrum,* 51, 1 (Spring 1975): 23.

[18] Leo Kisrow, *Leisure—A Challenge for the Church*, in *Spectrum,* 50, 1 (Spring 1974): 24.

[19] *American Heritage Dictionary of the English Language,* 1969 edition, s.v. "work."

[20] Evelyn Whitehead and James D. Whitehead, *Seasons of Strength,* Image Books (Garden City, NY: A Division of Doubleday and Co., 1986), 10.

[21] Stated in *Aging and the Search for Meaning*, in *Spiritual Maturity in the Later Years,* James Seeber, ed. (New York: Haworth Press, 1990), 113.

[22] Taken from Dry Salvages, in *T.S. Eliot: Collected Poems 1909–1962,* (New York: Harcourt, Brace Jovanovich, Inc. 1963), 194.

[23] One example: David Fisher, *Growing Old in America* (New York: Oxford University Press, 1977), 211.

[24] Jules Willing, *The Reality of Retirement: The Inner Experience of Becoming a Retired Person* (New York: William Morrow and Co., 1981), 220.

[25] Robert Butler and Herbert Gleason, eds., *Productive Aging* (New York: Spring Publishing Co., 1985), 83.

[26] Paul Maves, *Older People As Volunteers,* in *Centering,* IV 2 Summer 1987, 16.

[27] Arthur Becker, *Ministry with Older Persons* (Minneapolis, MN: Augsburg Publishing House, 1986), 83.

12. Reading Literary Gems

[1] Thomas Cole and Sally Gadow, eds., *What Does It Mean to Grow Old?* (Durham: Duke University Press, 1986), 39.

[2] Donald Deffner, *The Compassionate Mind: Theological Dialogue with the Educated* (St. Louis: Concordia Publishing House, 1990), 114–119.

[3] Susan Tamke in her research on the elderly as depicted in nursery literature gives reference to visual characteristics of shrivelled skin, wrinkles, loss of teeth, harshness of voice, etc., as an author's deliberate punishment for unwanted behavior. "Human Values and Aging: The Perspective of the Victorian Nursery," in *Aging and the Elderly* (Atlantic Highlands, N.J.: Humanities Press, 1978), 70.

[4] Lance Gentile and Merna McMillan, *Reading: A Means of Renewal for the Aged,* in *Educational Gerontology*. 4, 3 (July-September 1979):215–222.

[5] Ibid. 218.

[6] Elizabeth Canham, *Simplify, Simplify,* in *Weavings: A Journal of the Christian Spiritual Life*. V, 3 (May/June, 1990): 25.

[7] Hugo Munsterberg, *The Crown of Life: Artistic Creativity in Old Age* (San Diego: Harcourt Brace Jovanovich Inc., 1983), 207.

[8] Perry Gresham, *With Wings As Eagles* (South Yarmouth, MA: John Curley & Associates, 1980), chapter 1.

[9] Henri Nouwen and Walter Gaffney, *Aging, the Fulfillment of Life* (Garden City, NY: Doubleday & Co., 1976), 13.

[10] Douglas Steere, *Prayer and Worship* (Richmond, IN: Friends University Press, 1978), 52.

[11] The New Oxford Annotated Bible, Ecclesiastes 3: 1–8.

13. Caregiving as an Active Christian Affair

[1] Thomas B. Robb, *Growing Up: Pastoral Nurture for the Later Years* (New York: Haworth Press, 1991), 114.

[2] Ibid., 114–118.

[3] Ibid., 116.

[4] Dianne Springer and Timothy H. Brubaker, *Family Caregivers and Dependent Elderly* (Beverly Hills: Sage Publications, 1984), 14.

[5] Robb, 106–114.

[6] Springer, 18.

[7] Bruce Vladeck, *Unloving Care: The Nursing Home Tragedy* (New York: Basic Books Inc., 1980), 149.

[8] Doris Lessing, *The Diary of a Good Neighbor,* in *The Diaries of Jane Somers* (New York: Vintage Books. A division of Random House, 1984).

[9] Jo Horne, *A Survival Guide for Family Caregivers* (Minneapolis: CompCare Publications, 1991), chapter 1.

[10] William Hendricks, *A Theology of Aging* (Nashville: Broadman Press, 1986), 166.

[11] Tilman Smith, *In Favor of Growing Older* (Scottsdale, PA: Herald Press, 1981), 152.

[12] Henri J. Nouwen, *Care and the Elderly,* in *Aging and the Human Spirit, a Reader in Religion and Gerontology,* Second edition, Carol LeFevre and Perry LeFevre, eds., 323.

[13] Ibid., 325.

[14] James Ellor, *Wholistic Theology As a Conceptual Foundation for Services for the Oldest Old,* in *Spiritual Maturity in the Later Years,* James Seeber, ed. (New York: Haworth Press, 1990), 103.

[15] Ken Dychtwald, *Age Wave* (Los Angeles: Jeremy Tarcher, 1989), 157–171.

[16] Albert Myers and Christopher P. Andersen, *Success Over Sixty* (Boston: G.K. Hall & Co., 1985), 222.

[17] Robert Gray and David Moberg, *The Church and the Older Person,* rev. edition (Grand Rapids, MI.: William B. Eerdmans Publishing Co., 1977), 185–186.

[18] Martin Marty, *Cultural Antecedents to Attitudes toward Aging,* in *Ministry with the Aging* William Clements, ed. (Cambridge: Harper & Row, 1981), 72.

[19] Carole Haber, *Beyond Sixty-Five: The Dilemma of Old Age in America's Past* (Cambridge: Cambridge University Press, 1983), 5.

[20] Ibid., 129.

[21] Perry LeFevre, *Toward a Theology of Aging,* in *Aging and the Human Spirit: A Reader in Religion and Gerontology,* 2nd ed., Carol

LeFevre and Perry LeFevre, eds. (Chicago: Exploration Press, 1981), 47.

[22] Maggie Kuhn, in *Maggie Kuhn on Aging: A Dialogue,* Dieter Hessel, ed. (Philadelphia: Westminster Press, 1977), 114.

[23] Arthur Becker, *Ministry with Older Persons: A Guide for Clergy and Congregations* (Minneapolis: Augsburg Publishing House, 1986), 137.

[24] Christine K. Cassel, *The Meaning of Health Care in Old Age,* in *What Does It Mean to Grow Old?* Thomas Cole, Sally Gadow, eds. (Durham, NC: Duke University Press, 1986) 187.

[25] Ibid., 188.

[26] Ibid., 191.

[27] Mary Gordan, *Final Payments* (New York: Random House, 1978).

[28] An example of one program: in Peggy Eastman and Annette Kane's *Respite: Guidelines for a Program Whose Time is Now,* sponsored by the National Council of Catholic Women. Washington, D.C.: 1986.

[29] Margaret J. Rinck, *Can Christians Love Too Much?* (Grand Rapids, MI: Zondervan Publishing House, 1989).

[30] Springer, 42–54.

[31] A lengthy list describing the term "caring congregation" can be found on p. 67 of Harold Wilke's *Re-creating A Caring Congregation,* written with a focus on disability.

[32] Hendricks, *A Theology for Aging.*

[33] G. Gordon Harris, *God and the Elderly: Biblical Perspectives on Aging* (Philadelphia: Fortress Press, 1987), 111.

[34] Barbara Myerhoff, *Number Our Days* (New York: Simon & Schuster, 1978), 252.

14. Advocacy

[1] Arthur Becker, *Ministry with Older Persons* (Minneapolis: Augsburg Publishing House, 1986), 196.

[2] Mary Winters, *Congregational and Individual Advocacy on Aging,* in *Older Adult Ministry* (Atlanta: Presbyterian Publishing House, 1987), 195.

[3] *Oxford Book of Prayer,* George Appleton, ed. (New York: Oxford University Press, 1988), 113.

15. Celebrating Age as Rebirth of Wonder

[1] Paul Pruyser, *Aging: Downward, Upward or Forward?*, in *Toward A Theology of Aging,* Seward Hiltner, guest ed. (New York: Human Sciences Press, 1979). Special issue of *Pastoral Psychology* 24 (Winter 1975): 102–117.

[2] Henry Simmons, *Countering Cultural Metaphors of Aging,* in *Spiritual Maturity in Later Years,* James Seeber, ed. (New York: Haworth Press, 1990), 157–164.

[3] *Union Leader,* Manchester, New Hampshire, Feb. 29, 1992. p. 10 Obituary. *Guiness Book of World Records* had declared her the oldest living American.

[4] Ronald Blythe, *The View in Winter* (New York: Harcourt Brace Jovanovich Inc., 1979), 265.

[5] Barbara Myerhoff, *Number Our Days,* A Touchstone Book (New York: Simon & Schuster, 1980), 10.

[6] Urban Holmes, *Worship and Aging: Memory and Repentance*, in *Ministry with the Aging* William Clements, ed. (Cambridge: Harper & Row, 1981), 106.

SELECTED BIBLIOGRAPHY

Alexander, Jo, et al., eds. *Women and Aging: An Anthology by Women*. Corvallis, OR: Calyx Books, 1991.

Arts, the Humanities and Older Americans: A Catalog of Program Profiles. Washington, D.C.: National Council On Aging, 1981.

Beauvoir, Simone de. *The Coming of Age*. New York: G.P. Putnam's Sons, 1972.

Becker, Arthur. *Ministry with Older Persons*. Minneapolis: Augsburg Publishing House, 1986.

Bell, Marilyn, ed. *Women as Elders: The Feminist Politics of Aging*. New York.: Harrington Park Press, 1986.

Belsky, Janet. *The Psychology of Aging*. Monterey, CA: Brooks/Cole Publishing Co., 1984.

Bender, David, ed. *The Elderly: Opposing Viewpoints*. San Diego, CA: Greenhaven Press, 1990.

Berman, Phillip, ed. *The Courage to Grow Old*. New York: Ballentine Books, 1988.

Bianchi, Eugene. *Aging as a Spiritual Journey.* New York: Crossroad, 1990.

Blythe, Ronald. *The View in Winter.* New York: Harcourt Brace Jovanovich, 1979.

Boyle, Sarah-Patton. *The Desert Blooms.* Nashville: Abingdon Press, 1983.

Bridges, William. *Transitions: Making Sense of Life's Changes.* Reading, MA: Addison-Wesley, 1980.

Butler, Robert and Herbert Gleason, eds. *Productive Aging: Enhancing Vitality in Later Life.* New York: Springer Publishing Co., 1985.

————. *Why Survive? Being Old in America.* New York: Harper & Row, 1985.

Carroll, L. Patrick and Katherine Marie Dyckman. *Chaos or Creation: The Spirituality in Mid-Life.* New York/Mahwah: Paulist Press, 1986.

Clements, William, ed. *Ministry with the Aging.* Cambridge: Harper & Row, 1981.

Cluff, Claudia B. *The Frail in Our Midst.* Trenton, NJ: Episcopal Diocese of New Jersey, 1982.

Cole, Thomas and Sally Gadow, eds. *What Does it Mean to Grow Old? Reflections from the Humanities.* Durham, NC: Duke University Press, 1986.

Cottin, Lou. *Elders in Rebellion: A Guide To Senior Activism.* Garden City, NY: Anchor Press/Doubleday, 1979.

Coupland, Susan. *Beginning to Pray in Old Age.* Cambridge: Cowley Press, 1985.

DelBene, Ron, et al. *When An Aging Loved One Needs Care.* Nashville: Upper Room Books, 1991.

Dulin, Rachel. *A Crown of Glory: A Biblical View of Aging.* New York: Paulist Press, 1988.

Dychtwald, Ken. *Age Wave.* Los Angeles: Jeremy Tarcher, 1989.

Elliot, Elisabeth. *Forget Me Not: Loving God's Aging Children.* Portland, OR: Multnomah Press, 1989.

Episcopal Society for Ministry on Aging. *Affirmative Aging: A Resource for Ministry*. [n.p.] ESMA, 1985.

Erikson, Erik, Joan Erikson, and Helen Kivnick. *Vital Involvement in Old Age*. New York: W.W. Norton, 1986.

Farber, Norma. *How Does it Feel to be Old?* New York: Dutton, 1979.

Fischer, David H. *Growing Old in America: The Bland-Lee Lectures Delivered at Clark University.* New York: Oxford University Press, 1977.

Fischer, Edward. *Life in the Afternoon*. New York: Paulist Press, 1987.

Fischer, Kathleen. *Winter Grace: Spirituality for the Later Years.* Mahwah, NJ: Paulist Press, 1985.

Fischer, Lucy and Kay Schaffer,. *Older Volunteers.* Newbury Park, CA: Sage Publications, 1993.

Fowler, Margaret and Priscilla McCutcheon. *Songs of Experience: An Anthology of Literature on Growing Old.* New York: Ballantine Books, 1991.

Gerber, Jerry, et al. *Lifetrends: The Future of Baby Boomers and Other Aging Americans.* New York: Macmillan Publishing Co., 1989.

Gray, Robert M. and David Moberg. *The Church and the Older Person.* Rev. ed. Grand Rapids, MI: William B. Eerdmans Publishing Co., 1977.

Gray, Ruth. *Survival of the Spirit: My Detour through a Retirement Home.* Atlanta: John Knox Press, 1985.

Gresham, Perry. *With Wings As Eagles.* South Yarmouth, MA: John Curley and Associates, Inc., 1980.

Griggs, Donald and Judy M. Walther. *Christian Education in the Small Church.* Valley Forge: Judson Press, 1988.

Haber, Carole. *Beyond Sixty-Five: The Dilemma of Old Age in America's Past.* Cambridge: Cambridge University Press, 1983.

Harris, J. Gordon. *Biblical Perspectives on Aging.* Philadelphia: Fortress Press, 1987.

Haugk, Kenneth. *Christian Caregiving.* Minneapolis: Augsburg Pub. House, 1984.

Hessel, Dieter. *Maggie Kuhn on Aging: A Dialogue.* Philadelphia: Westminster Press, 1977.

Hiltner, Seward, ed. *Toward a Theology of Aging.* New York: Human Sciences Press, 1975.

Holland, Joe. *Creative Communion: Toward a Spirituality of Work.* New York: Paulist Press, 1989.

Horne, Jo and Leo Baldwin. *Home-Sharing and Other Lifestyle Options.* AARP Book. Glenview, Ill.: Scott, Foresman and Co., 1988.

———. *A Survival Guide for Family Caregivers.* Minneapolis: CompCare Publishers, 1991.

Hulme, William. *Vintage Years: Growing Older with Meaning and Hope.* Philadelphia: Westminster, 1986.

Hutchison, Frank. *Aging Comes of Age.* Louisville: Westminster/John Knox Press, 1991.

Jackson, James, et al. *Aging in Black America.* Newbury Park CA: Sage Publications, 1992.

Jacobs, Ruth Harriet. *Be An Outrageous Older Woman. A RASP. (A Remarkable, Aging, Smart, Person).* Manchester, CT: Knowledge, Ideas and Trends Publishers, 1991.

———. *Older Women, Surviving and Thriving: A Manual for Group Leaders.* Milwaukee: Family Service America, 1987.

Johnson, Susanne. *Christian Spiritual Formation in the Church and Classroom.* Nashville: Abingdon Press, 1989.

Jones, Alan. *Exploring Spiritual Direction: An Essay on Christian Friendship.* San Francisco CA: Harper, 1982.

Kerr, Horace. *How to Minister to Senior Adults in Your Church.* Nashville: Broadman Press, 1980.

Kornhaber, Arthur and Kenneth Woodward. *Grandparents/*

Grandchildren: The Vital Connection. Garden City, NY: Doubleday/Anchor, 1981.

Landau, Elaine. *Growing Old in America.* New York: Julian Messner, 1985.

Langone, John. *Growing Older: What Young People Should Know.* Boston: Little, Brown, 1991.

Larimore, Helen. *Older Women in Recovery.* Deerfield Beach, FL: Health Communications, 1992.

Leaf, Alexander. "Every Day Is A Gift When You Are Over 100," *National Geographic.* 143 (January 1973): 92-119.

LeFevre, Carol and Perry LeFevre, eds. *Aging and the Human Spirit: A Reader in Religion and Gerontology.* 2 ed. Chicago: Exploration Press, 1981.

LeShan, Eda. *Grandparents: A Special Kind of Love.* New York: Macmillan Publishing Co., 1984.

Lessing, Doris. *The Diaries of Jane Somers.* New York: Vintage Books, 1984.

Lesnoff-Caravaglia, Gari. *The World of the Older Woman: Conflicts and Resolutions.* New York: Human Sciences Press, 1984.

Lyon, Brynolf. *Toward a Practical Theology of Aging.* Philadelphia: Fortress, 1985.

MacDonald, Barbara with Cynthia Rich *Look Me in the Eye.* San Francisco: Spinsters Book Co., 1990.

Maclay, Elise. *Green Winter: Celebrations of Old Age.* New York: Readers Digest Press, 1977.

Maitland, David. *Looking Both Ways: A Theology for Mid-Life.* Atlanta: John Knox Press, 1985.

———. *Aging: A Time for New Learning.* Atlanta: John Knox Press, 1987.

———. *Aging as Counterculture: A Vocation for the Later Years.* New York: Pilgrim Press, 1991.

Manning, Doug. *When Loves Gets Tough: The Nursing Home Decision.* Hereford, TX: InSight Books, 1991.

Martz, Sandra, ed. *When I Am An Old Woman I Shall Wear Purple.* Manhattan Beach, CA: Papier-Maché Press, 1987.

Maves, Paul. *Older Volunteers in Church and Community.* Valley Forge: Judson Press, 1981.

Merriam, Sharon. *Themes of Adulthood through Literature.* New York: Teachers College Press, 1983.

Meyer, William. *Nice Things about Growing Older.* Meditations. Brea, CA: Educational Ministries, 1990.

Miller, Sigmund. *Conquest of Aging: Definitive Home Medical Reference.* New York: Collier Books, 1986.

Morgan, Richard. *No Wrinkles on the Soul.* A Book of Readings for Older Adults. Nashville: Upper Room Books, 1990.

Myerhoff, Barbara. *Number Our Days* New York: Simon & Schuster, 1980.

Murphy, James. *Concepts of Leisure. Philosophical Implications.* Englewood Cliffs, NJ: Prentice-Hall, 1974.

Nelson, C. Ellis. *How Faith Matures.* Louisville, KY: Westminster/John Knox Press, 1989.

Neugarten, Bernice, ed. *Middle Age and Aging: Reader in Social Psychology.* Chicago: University of Chicago Press, 1968.

Nouwen, Henri. *Aging.* Garden City, NY: Doubleday, 1974.

Ochs, Carol. *Women and Spirituality.* Totowa, NJ: Rowman & Allanheld, 1983.

Older Adult Ministry: A Resource for Program Development. Joint venture of Episcopal Society for Ministry on Aging, the Presbyterian Office on Aging, United Church Board for Homeland Ministries. Atlanta: Presbyterian Publishing House, 1987.

Painter, Charlotte. *Gifts of Age: Portraits and Essays of 32 Remarkable Women*. San Francisco: Chronicle Books, 1985.

Pieper, Josef. *Leisure: The Basis of Culture.* New York: Pantheon Books, 1952.

Pierskella, Carol. *Rehearsal for Retirement.* Valley Forge, PA: National Ministries, American Baptist Churches, USA, 1992.

Polacco, Patricia. *Mrs. Katz & Tush.* New York: Bantam Little Rooster Book, 1992.

Porcino, Jane. *Growing Older, Getting Better.* Reading, MA: Addison-Wesley Publishing, 1983.

Reynolds, Lillian R. *No Retirement: Devotions on Christian*

Discipleship for Older People. Philadelphia: Fortress Press, 1984.

Robb, Thomas B. *Growing Up: Pastoral Nurture for the Later Years.* New York: Haworth Press, 1991.

Sapp, Stephen. *Full of Years. Aging and the Elderly in the Bible and Today.* Nashville: Abingdon Press, 1987.

Sarton, May. *As We Are Now.* New York: W.W. Norton, 1973.

———. *At Seventy.* New York: W.W. Norton, 1984.

Seeber, James J., ed. *Spiritual Maturity in the Later Years.* New York: Haworth Press, 1990.

Silverstone, Barbara. *You and Your Aging Parents.* New York: Pantheon Books, 1976.

Skinner, B.F. and M.E. Vaughan. *Enjoy Old Age: A Program of Self-Management.* New York: W.W. Norton, 1983.

Smith, Tilman. *In Favor of Growing Older.* Scottsdale, PA: Herald Press, 1991.

Spicker, Stuart, Kathleen Woodward and David Van Tassel, eds. *Aging and the Elderly: Humanistic Perspectives in Gerontology.* Atlantic Highlands, NJ: Humanities Press, 1978.

Spinnelli, Eileen. *Somebody Loves You, Mr. Hatch.* New York: Bradbury Press, 1991.

Springer, Dianne. *Family Caregivers and Dependent Elderly.* Sage Human Services Guide 38. Beverly Hills: Sage Publications, 1984.

Stafford, Tim. *As Our Years Increase.* New York: Harper, 1989.

Stagg, Frank. *The Bible Speaks on Aging.* Nashville: Broadman Press, 1981.

Sullender, R. Scott. *Losses in Later Life: A New Way of Walking with God.* New York: Paulist Press/Integration Books, 1989.

Super, Gretchen. *What Kind of Family Do You Have?* Frederick, MD: Twenty-First Century Books, 1991.

Syverson, Betty. *Bible Readings for Caregivers.* Minneapolis: Augsburg Publishing House, 1987.

Szentkeresti, Karen Ann and Jeanne Tighe. *Rethinking Adult Religious Education.* New York/Mahwah: Paulist Press, 1986.

Taylor, Blaine. *The Church's Ministry with Older Adults.* Nashville: Abingdon Press, 1984.

Tobin, Sheldon. *Enabling the Elderly.* Albany: State University of New York Press, 1986.

Tournier, Paul. *Learn to Grow Old.* Louisville, KY: Westminster/John Knox Press, 1983.

Van Tassel, David, ed. *Aging, Death and Completion of Being.* [n.p.]: University of Pennsylvania Press, 1979.

Vogel, Linda. *The Religious Education of Older Adults.* Birmingham, AL: Religious Education Press, 1984.

————. *Teaching Older Adults: A Guide For Teachers and Leaders.* Nashville: Discipleship Resources, 1989.

Westerhoff, John H. and William Willimon. *Liturgy and Learning through the Life Cycle.* New York: Seabury Press, 1980.

Whitehead, Evelyn E. and James D. *Seasons of Strength:* New Visions of Adult Christian Maturing. Garden City, NY: Doubleday, 1986.

Willing, Jules. *The Reality of Retirement: The Inner Experience of Becoming a Retired Person.* New York: William Morrow, 1981.

Yates, Elizabeth. *Up the Golden Stair.* New York: E.P. Dutton & Co., 1966.

Zimmerman, William. *How to Tape Instant Oral Biographies.* New York: Guarcionex Press, 1979.

Seuss, Dr. *You're Only Old Once.* New York: Random House, 1986.